After Haggerty

It can be a daunting experience for a man to move into a new home in some kind of attempt to escape the deadlocks of his past, only to find his life dominated by the deadlocked past of the previous occupants. Soon after moving into the London flat he has rented from Haggerty, Bernard Link is faced with the arrival of Claire. For Claire, Bernard's unexpected presence in the flat is part of the aftermath of Haggerty, like her baby son and her bitter memories. For Bernard, a drama critic in his forties (with two failed marriages behind him), Claire's presence mirrors his own position. He is caught between his half-guilty sense of political impotence and his half-guilty resentment of his own ill-educated father's narrowness.

First presented at the Aldwych Theatre by the Royal Shakespeare Company February 26 1970, David Mercer's play focuses sharply on the agonies of two individuals whose dilemmas interlock.

The photograph on the front cover shows Frank Finlay, Billie Dixon and Leslie Sands in a scene from the Royal Shakespeare Company's production. This and the photograph of David Mercer on the back of the cover are reproduced by courtesy of Irving Teitelbaum.

D0970735

by the same author

THE GENERATIONS

THREE TV COMEDIES

RIDE A COCK HORSE

BELCHER'S LUCK

THE PARACHUTE

THE GOVERNOR'S LADY

ON THE EVE OF PUBLICATION AND OTHER PLAYS

FLINT

THE BANKRUPT AND OTHER PLAYS

DUCK SONG

HUGGY BEAR AND OTHER PLAYS

DAVID MERCER

After Haggerty

METHUEN & CO LTD
11 NEW FETTER LANE . LONDON EC4

First published 1970 *by Methuen & Co Ltd*
Reprinted 1978 *by Eyre Methuen Ltd*
11 New Fetter Lane
London EC4P 4EE

© 1970 *by David Mercer*
ISBN 0 413 39860 9

Printed in Great Britain by
Cox & Wyman Ltd., Fakenham, Norfolk.

After Haggerty

AFTER HAGGERTY was first presented at the Aldwych Theatre on February 26 1970 by the Royal Shakespeare Company with the following cast:

BERNARD LINK *45*	Frank Finlay
CLAIRE *late 20s*	Billie Dixon
CHRIS	John White
ROGER	David Wood
MR LINK	Leslie Sands
INTERPRETERS	Margo Jenkins
	Frederick Arle
	Helen Francois
ACTORS	Tim Curry
	Helen Francois
	Margo Jenkins
	Malcolm Kaye
UNDERTAKERS	Lewis Wilson
	Frederick Arle

Directed by David Jones
Designed by Alan Tagg

ACT ONE

Scene One

A big room with high windows, containing only a few sheeted chairs, a sheeted desk, two stepladders, pots of paint, etc. We hear a woman's voice, American, after a loud beating on the door. This is CLAIRE, *a bonily attractive woman in her late twenties.*

CLAIRE (*off*). Haggerty. You there? You *in* there? (*Pause.*) You *are* in there, you bastard. (*Pause.*) I can shout louder than this. As you know. (*Pause.*) Haggerty?

> *The banging on the door starts again, louder. A tall, fattish Englishman of forty-five enters from another door. This is* BERNARD. *The banging stops.*

CLAIRE. Haggerty, if you don't open up I shall push your goddam baby through the keyhole. I've got it here. In one of those kiddy chairs. (*Pause.*) Haggerty? Your child is shitting. (*Pause.*) Listen. I'm going to cram kid and shit right through your keyhole. Do you hear me, crabhead?

> BERNARD *is very upset by all this. Slowly, he goes to the door – and cautiously opens it.* CLAIRE *blasts into the room, but is naturally, since expecting* HAGGERTY, *somewhat taken aback at the sight of* BERNARD.

BERNARD. I'm not Haggerty.

CLAIRE. Prove it.

BERNARD. Well, I –

CLAIRE. Look. Let's get this straight. It's obvious at once your mind is kind of sluggish. And mine is *fast*. My mental processes go *whoosh*. Therefore, I know you are not Haggerty, but you're already under sentence. *You're* going to catch a big hunk of the aggression I've been working up from New York to that goddam door. And I'll tell you this. This is a fact. That was *Haggerty's* door. Once. (*Pause.*) And mine.

CLAIRE *stands looking round.* BERNARD *is somewhat trauma-tized and sinks on to one of the dust-sheeted chairs.*

Having the place done up?

BERNARD. Yes, I –

CLAIRE. Yeah. I saw, out in the square. The district sure is *going up.* (*Pause.*) Don't tell me. I'm cunning. I know. Haggerty leased you the apartment. Huh?

BERNARD. Yes. (*Pause.*) I've only been here a week.

CLAIRE. So you *know* Haggerty. I mean, I just want to know *how much* I'm confusing you.

BERNARD. No. His lawyer –

CLAIRE. Haggerty has lawyers now? Jesus. That's ironic. My lawyers have never managed to have *Haggerty.* If you knew him that would not surprise you.

BERNARD. I'm just a –

CLAIRE. Just a what? And just a who? But let me inform you before you go on to the defensive that you are the kind of Englishman I really hate. London is full of you. If human society was logical, you wouldn't have a name you'd have a number.

BERNARD. My name's Link. Bernard.

CLAIRE. I know why you're looking at me like that. You're wondering: is there anything human in that woman? Anything warm? Gentle? Kind? Reasonable? Anything *not* aggressive?

BERNARD. I –

CLAIRE. I can reliably inform you it's all there. But you have to work for it. Do you like that kind of work?

BERNARD (*pointing doorwards*). The baby?

CLAIRE. *Be* clever! *Strike* at the maternal areas! And you'll bust your chubby knuckles.

She goes to the window and looks out.

This used to be a real crummy square. Now look at it! Plum

doors. White façades. (*Pause.*) Do I see a coach lantern over there on the other side? (*Pause.*) Do I see a fairy peeping out from behind one of those polystyrene sculptures?

BERNARD. There are still a lot of poor families.

CLAIRE. Are there? Are there really? So I suppose you can still feel pretty good. Feel like you haven't *gone up too far*. (*Pause.*) I can see you have a real tender conscience throbbing somewhere inside that large bag of fat!

Pause.

BERNARD. The baby –

CLAIRE. Leave the baby to me, Bernard. Bernard Link. Christ! Link! Did the other kids at school call you Missing? Don't answer. I realize you're bound to've heard it before.

BERNARD. You said the baby was –

CLAIRE. Shitting?

Pause.

BERNARD. Yes.

CLAIRE. Do you wish to intervene? Have you got some ingenious scheme to prevent his rotten little bowels doing what physiology makes inevitable?

Pause.

BERNARD. He's very quiet.

CLAIRE. I'll say for Haggerty's kid, he shits quietly. He gets contemplative. If he could think, he would be thinking: wait till she gets a whiff of *this* one!

BERNARD. When I came in this morning. With my groceries. There were three small children standing there staring at me. Quite unnerving. (*Pause.*) Well, I smiled. As one does. A friendly little smile for the small people. Who stare at you. (*Pause.*) And the girl – she couldn't have been more than six – said: Hello, fat man.

CLAIRE *crosses to him.*

CLAIRE. Are you a defeated person?

Pause.

BERNARD. No.

CLAIRE. So why didn't you kick her in the pussy?

Pause.

BERNARD. That would have been . . . disproportionate to the offence.

CLAIRE. You figured that out so quick with *your* mind? With the urge to kick out still embryonic?

Pause.

BERNARD. I think you've jumped to hasty conclusions about my mind. (*Pause.*) I resent that.

There is a loud yell from the baby outside. CLAIRE *goes out.* BERNARD *sits wondering things to himself. The baby's cries get louder, and go on for about half a minute.* CLAIRE *returns with a large bundle of Kleenex in one fist. The baby stops crying.*

CLAIRE. There it is.

BERNARD. I wish you wouldn't –

CLAIRE. You don't wish to know about Rass's crap? After what he's put into it, I mean? (*Pause.*) All that effort. All those thousands of articulated functions functioning? (*Pause.*) You're going to reject him?

BERNARD. Well. He hasn't met me. Has he?

CLAIRE. He and I don't like being in the same room as each other. Young as he is, we have arrived through God knows what primitive means of communication at this pact: we try to avoid each other. Since the child can't walk, on me falls the responsibility of respecting our wishes.

Pause.

BERNARD. What a curious name. Rass.

CLAIRE. His name, given its full credit of syllables, is Raskolnikov.

BERNARD. My God.

CLAIRE. Yes. It's worse than you being called Link. It knocks Link into a cocked hat. It makes Link sound unimaginative, and safe, and –

BERNARD. Children tend not to be familiar with questions of human evolution. It's only adults who've always said, I mean

some of them: ha ha! I expect you were called Missing at
school.

CLAIRE. So I'm glad you never suffered in that respect. May
I now flush Rass's de-nurtured chicken purée down the
john?

BERNARD. Yes. I wish you would.

CLAIRE. If you'd flown from New York to London at six months
to find no father and a stranger in your apartment – *your* little
turds would reach a new high in whatever goes for decibels in
smell.

BERNARD. He doesn't know there's a stranger in the, the flat.

CLAIRE. I think I overwhelm you, Bernard.

She exits through the other door with the mass of tissue.
BERNARD *muses.*

BERNARD. Raskolnikov. Raskolnikov Haggerty.

He goes through the door to the hall. The child starts crying.
Fade out and fade in to

Scene Two

The stage is dark. An illuminated sign is lowered saying: BUDAPEST.
A single spot picks out BERNARD *standing downstage centre. Another*
spot picks out an INTERPRETER *standing just behind him, left.*
BERNARD *holds in one hand a small card of notes. He seems shy and*
humble, but speaks firmly. There are very faint and far sporadic
bursts of submachine gun fire.

BERNARD. This lecture was of course organized at a moment
when the recent developments in your country had not reached
the brink of outward, historical expression. (*Pause.*) I am
amazed and confused to be here at such a critical time. (*Pause.*)
And needless to say, I am grateful – and indeed humble – to find
so many of you present this evening.

The INTERPRETER *comes forward and repeats what he has said*
in Hungarian. She then resumes her former position.

To confront you as a drama critic from England is one thing.
To confront you as a Marxist as well, may be to invite your
justifiable derision. (*Pause.*) Returning to the question of the
work of Christopher Fry and John Whiting –

> *There is a sudden and tremendous burst of machine gun fire off.*
> *The* BUDAPEST *sign is raised, as the spots on* BERNARD *and the*
> INTERPRETER *fade.*
> *Darkness whilst* BERNARD *removes his jacket and tie, and un-*
> *buttons his shirt cuffs.*
> *Fade up* BERNARD *pulling forward a chair. He sits down,*
> *fastening his shirt cuffs. Spot on* BERNARD.

What about that, then, dad? Yes. Bloody well nearly killed, I
was. (*Long pause.*) No. *Hungary, dad.* (*Pause.*) No, dad. Tito –
he's Jugoslavia. (*Pause.*) Looking at your face I'd say you're
entirely unmoved by the information I might have been killed.
(*Pause.*) *What's* that? We'd never have got me Auntie Bertha
over there for the funeral? (*Pause.*) Yes, I know I'm alive and
well and you're entitled to your little joke. Ha Ha. (*Points.*)
See that raincoat? There's a *bullet* hole in the sleeve of that raincoat. (*Pause.*) No. *Nobody* was shooting at me. I just got in the
bloody way. And should you recount the horrendous tale to
Auntie Bertha, you might as well add they don't go in for funeral
ham teas in Hungary either. (*Pause.*) I was just having my little
joke, dad. (*Pause.*) She's what? Having a varicose vein removed? (*Pause.*) Listen. (*Shouts.*) I nearly had my bloody life
removed. Yes. My *existence.* Wiped out. (*Pause.*) You know.
You have this habit. And it irritates me. Every time I tell you
something that happens to *me* – you slap your thigh and say:
eh, bloody hell, what'll happen next!

> BERNARD *stands and takes his tie from his pocket, begins to put*
> *it on.*

I'll send you a map, dad. With a thick red ring drawn round
Hungary. You might spend a minute or two with it between
work and your allotment. (*Pause.*) If I don't get off now I'll
never catch that train at Leeds. (*Pause.*) Yes, I know you never

see me more than one day a century. Yes, I know. (*Pause.*) Well,
I'm just going upstairs to pack.

Fade out and fade in to

Scene Three

BERNARD *sits at the desk, now cleared of its dust-sheet, and loaded
with books, papers and a typewriter. He is typing.*
At the window, two young men, CHRIS *and* ROGER, *are painting the
window frame.* ROGER *stops, with his brush poised.*

ROGER. By the way, Bernard. I can't make it here tomorrow.

BERNARD. Oh? Why?

ROGER. I've got an audition.

BERNARD. Where?

ROGER. Watford. Isn't it beastly.

BERNARD. The part, or the act of desertion?

ROGER. I'll die if I don't get something.

    Pause.

BERNARD. There are bound to be hazards if one goes to a firm
that employs out-of-work actors.

ROGER. Can't think why you did, love.

    CHRIS *stops painting and goes to* BERNARD.

CHRIS. I'm not an actor. Nor a pouf neither.

ROGER. Chrissy – stop it! And be careful, you're getting wiggly
paint marks all down the back of your hand. *You're* not a pro-
fessional. Selling cars *he* was last week. Shouldn't be surprised
they were you-know-what cars, either.

CHRIS (*to* BERNARD). I'm just telling you. That's all.

    CHRIS *goes back to the window.* BERNARD *wearily turns for the
    inevitable chat.*

BERNARD. My last flat, it was anarchists.

ROGER. Smelly old lot!

BERNARD. They weren't as bad as actors. (*Pause.*) They were a
bit of a trial though. (*Pause.*) They painted half the place, then
disappeared. For ever.

ROGER. And of course – you'd paid them, dear, hadn't you? Silly old you.

BERNARD. I'd paid them half. (*Pause.*) Wherever they are, I suppose they can at least feel they kept their integrity. Half for half. (*Pause.*) I liked them, actually. I mean, for one thing they were terribly tidy and clean. (*Pause.*) One of them was sort of mad. (*Pause.*) They were very kind to him. And did most of his share. (*Pause.*) One day he forgot to wash his hands and just wiped the paint off on the towels in the bathroom. (*Pause.*) Two of them led him off somewhere and talked to him quietly. The other chap washed the dirty towels. (*Pause.*) He didn't actually get all the paint out. But I was touched by the gesture. (*Pause.*) They were all convinced mad people shouldn't be put in mental hospitals, and they looked after William like a baby. (*Pause.*) What's more, their William had a First in mathematics at Cambridge.

ROGER. Drive anybody mad, wouldn't it? All those sums! (*Pause.*) And talking of babies –

BERNARD. Look, I've got work to do.

ROGER. Yes, I know you have, love. I read that piece of yours about Brecht in Berlin and I thought it was fabulous. *But.*

CHRIS. He had a row with your friend upstairs this morning.

ROGER. I wouldn't exactly call it a row. It was the baby, Bernard. What I mean, I went into the loo for a pee. And I had this bottle of turps in my hand. Ever so absent-minded. Well, I put it on the ledge whilst I made my little contribution to the London sewage authority; and well, of course I nip away forgetting all about me turps, don't I? Well, with my luck *she* goes in there with what's-his-name. I forgot to tell you I hadn't put the screw on the bottle in the first place. And well, dearie – it's turps all over the little daemon's head, isn't it? The clumsy bitch knocked it over, and –

CHRIS. I wish you'd belt up.

ROGER. Chrissy, I shall sulk. Shan't I, Bernard?

CHRIS. You do lay it on a bit thick, you know.

ROGER. When you're as sensitive as I am, cherub, there's no point laying it on thin. Every nasty crude remark from people like you becomes a positive *spear*. As for Madam Haggerty, a spot of turps, I said, won't do it any harm. You can tell she loathes it, so why go all primaternal-donna over a drop of white spirit?

BERNARD. I'm paying you to paint a few bloody walls, Roger. That's all. I don't even ask for colours, which God knows you'd argue about till doomsday. Just a few walls. Whilst I get on with my trashy occupation of writing endless rubbish about the endless rubbish people like you want to act in. (*Pause.*) *Act!*

ROGER. Did I *ask* to be burdened with the absurd lust for it? Did I? (*Pause.*) I mean, I have to tell you, Bernard, and I'm not one for evasion – that is not a baby up there. It is a surviving miscarriage. You can put me through the door, dear, if you like. *But.* Christ. Raskolnikov! I'm not one to pass up a giggle in *any* circumstances. *But.* I expect when Madame first saw it, it was all blood and mucous and all that ghastly stuff that comes out *with* these things. And she thought it was normal. Then they wash the poor little mite and she takes one look and what comes into her mind, I ask you: Dostoevsky!

BERNARD. It's a perfectly normal baby. So get going with your brush and shut up.

ROGER. In all honesty, Bernard. Could you say it's a perfectly normal *mother*? Showers the object with turpentine, then blames me! I mean I've heard some pretty vivid language in my time. Frankly I turned red. Me!

CHRIS. Why don't you mind your own business? Eh? I've never known such a gush of gab. Not even from the scores of queers I've known besides you. 'Course, what they do at the office, they make sure you get put on a job with some poor sod like me. All tongue-tied and hard-working. They know somebody's got to do the graft, don't they?

He goes to ROGER *and waves the paint-brush in his face.*

You're *old-fashioned, Rodge.* Did you know that? Imagine.

Old-fashioned at twenty-six. And do you know what's aged
you, sport? Your clacking tongue.

Taps ROGER'S *head.*

What you got in there? A bloody pianola?

Pause.

ROGER. *Chrissy!*

ROGER *begins to dab furiously if ineffectually at the window
frame.* CHRIS *appeals to* BERNARD.

CHRIS. His sort – you can't deal with them. Know what I mean?
He makes me wish I was prejudiced. If I let him yap he bores
the arse off me. And if I spell out the odd home truth, then
what? He's *hurt!* Look at him. You can see the blood pourin'
out of his spiritual wounds. (*Pause.*) For god's sake I'm harmless
enough. Ignorant. Uneducated. (*Pause.*) But at least I can take
anything, can't I? Fairies, blacks, dykes, students –

ROGER *turns to him waspishly.*

ROGER. Place a tick against which noun is out of place in the
above four!

CHRIS *goes over to* BERNARD.

CHRIS. I knew Haggerty, you know.

Pause.

BERNARD. I think I'll move into a hotel.

Pause.

CHRIS. He was great.

Pause.

BERNARD. How?

Pause.

CHRIS. You know what I mean? A great bloke.

ROGER. Listen to that! There's insight for you! *There's* a fully-
rounded psychological portrait of Madam's lover boy! If that
one had passed the eleven-plus, we'd have a psychiatrist on our
hands now. Wouldn't we? Sock us the rest of it, Freud. Will
you?

CHRIS. I'll duff him yet, Bernard. I'll have to.

ROGER. I take it all back, Chrissy. I'm still upset, that's all. I just can't cope with women. I adore them, but I can't cope. And when they're toting round their grisly wee progeny, they make me scream. One daren't *think* of that child's future. Start off with the name Rasputin and where on *earth* does one end up?

BERNARD. Ras – kolnikov.

ROGER. Kolnikov, then. Is she mad? Was Haggerty mad? The naughty mystery man. Where is Haggerty?

BERNARD. He's in Paris. I had a telegram from him after I signed the lease. It said: For interior decoration, go to 'Rely-On'. So I came to 'Rely-On' – did I not? Without even knowing me, Haggerty understood that I have a weakness for the unconventional. I'm not the sort of person who has his plumbing done by plumbers, building by builders, painting by painters. Oh no. Not me. I have to give work to the underdog – yes? Layabout actors. Anarchists. Earnest sixth-formers financing relief for the latest area of global devastation. What is the consequence? Every time I'm foolish enough to change flats, I live for weeks in some of the most dangerous environments in the world, short of actual warfare. (*Pause.*) I suspect Haggerty is some kind of genius. What else explains his knowing that I am a monument of vulnerability through his *lawyers*? The telegram was a masterpiece. It combined perceptiveness with sheer malice to a degree I have rarely experienced. (*Pause.*) I am labouring to explain, Roger, that without Haggerty you and I would actually have never shared the rich experiences we've had this last week. I hope the thought chills you – dear.

    Pause.

ROGER. I didn't come here to be rebuked, Bernard. It's time for our nice cups of nescaff, I think. Bags me the Gnome.

CHRIS. The bleeding *Gnome*?

ROGER. Bernard knows what I mean. That gorgeous big lumpy mug with the green spots. I call it The Gnome.

CHRIS. Oh, Jesus!

ROGER. *You* are getting the black chipped one with the wonky handle and I hope it draws blood.

B

Exit ROGER.

BERNARD *and* CHRIS *exchange a long, sympathetic glance.*

CHRIS. There's no holding some of them any more. Is there?

CLAIRE *strides in, holding an empty turps bottle.*

CLAIRE. Where is he?

BERNARD. Who?

CLAIRE. Ginger nuts.

BERNARD. *Please*, Claire –

CLAIRE. If he was any other sex, I'd ram it up his ass.

BERNARD. Wouldn't you like some nescaff?

CLAIRE. Bernard, the epoch of sociology may have brought them into their own – but Roger is a goddam maniac! Turpentine and babies' hair do not mix, Bernard. Like it kind of seeps down into their goddam *eyes*, if you get me.

BERNARD. I've had children. In my time.

CLAIRE. You did? And you bathed them in petroleum by-products?

BERNARD. For God's sake, one always has accidents with children around.

CLAIRE. Listen. I want Rass to live. That kid's gonna grow up and take his fair share of the crap that's flying if it's the last thing I ever do. With Haggerty's genes and my post-natal care he's going to be evil down to the toenails. (*Pause.*) What I have in mind is something like a Hitler. Or a Borgia. And don't think if you hang round my neck looking pained I'm going to crack. I cracked when I met Haggerty. And as far as I'm concerned the rest of life with him has become a treasured wound. (*Pause.*) Do you understand psychology, Bernard?

BERNARD. Well, I think over the years I've acquired –

CLAIRE. Yes. So dig this, man. Psychology is what I'm allergic to. Don't try to encircle me with comprehension, Bernard, or I'll go for your ego's jugular. I hope I inspire fear. If I don't, it means you're a loser in the natural selection stakes. It took millions of years to make American women out of dinosaurs, and I for one have no intention of throwing that achievement in the face of the Almighty. (*She pauses to enjoy* BERNARD'S *evident paralysis.*)

BERNARD (*almost yelping*). Claire – this is *my flat*!

CLAIRE. You mean you're kinky about *property*? Or is it just the problem of tenure? I thought Europe still had a few *genuine* socialists left! I mean, you don't even need *blacks* to get your kids on the barricades! (*Pause.*) Are you in touch, Bernard?

Pause.

BERNARD. How long were you thinking of staying?

CLAIRE *surveys* CHRIS, *who has been standing transfixed.*

CLAIRE. Why doesn't he get on with his painting?

Now both BERNARD *and* CLAIRE *are looking at* CHRIS. *After a moment he goes to the window and resumes painting.*

You can move into my place on Long Island any time you like, Bernard. D'you know Amagansett? You'd like it. Those Atlantic breakers, they'd flip you over and shake you up and you'd feel as good as new.

BERNARD. But –

CLAIRE. And weekends, the psychiatrists settle in like locusts. You can't *move* for the amount of Nobel Prize material there is lying about on that sand.

BERNARD. What I'm trying to say –

CLAIRE. I'm not a colonizer. I'm an ejector. (*Pause.*) I thought bangle-bollocks was making coffee.

Pause.

BERNARD. I thought I lived in London, if you'll pardon me.

CLAIRE. You don't seem to catch on. If there were such a thing as the supernatural and he were dead – I'd be Haggerty's ghost. Man, I'm haunting the fink already. Just calm down, will you? I saw the look in your eyes yesterday. I saw the crawling thought behind those moist peepers of yours. That I might turn out to be a *lay*. (*Pause.*) Bernard, I'm positive you don't wish to be thought unsubtle?

ROGER *comes in with three cups of coffee on a tray. Ignoring*

CLAIRE *he gives one each to* BERNARD *and* CHRIS, *takes one himself. He holds the tray for a moment, then holds it out to* CLAIRE.

ROGER. I can't count.

CLAIRE *takes his nose between her thumb and forefinger. Squawking,* ROGER *drops his coffee.* CLAIRE *takes the tray from his other hand and holds it out to him. He takes it, and flounces out.* CLAIRE *looks at* BERNARD. *She reaches out and he automatically gives her his coffee.*

CLAIRE. Cheers.

Fade out as she drinks and in to

Scene Four

The stage is dark. An illuminated sign is lowered saying : MOSCOW. *A single spot picks out* BERNARD *standing downstage centre. Another spot picks out an* INTERPRETER *standing just behind him, left.*

BERNARD. The crucial development in our theatre in nineteen fifty-six was, as has been repeated and analysed ad nauseam: Osborne's LOOK BACK IN ANGER. (*Refers to notes card in his hand.*) At the Royal Court Theatre in London an entire generation seemed to have found its own vehement, articulate expression in the character of Jimmy Porter.

The INTERPRETER *comes one step forward and repeats what he has said in Russian. She resumes her former position.*

The spots on BERNARD *and the* INTERPRETER *begin to fade during his following speech, and his voice also dies away.*

Whether the artist consciously wishes it or not, his work often reflects the movements and currents of historical change. Of dialectical change –

Fade out spots on BERNARD *and* INTERPRETER, *as the* MOSCOW *sign is raised.*

Darkness whilst BERNARD *puts on a raincoat.*

Fade up BERNARD *pulling forward a chair and sitting down facing the audience.*

Yes, I know you gave me a key but I lost it. (*Looks at his watch.*) Made it up the M1 in just over three and a half hours this time. (*Pause.*) Well. When you weren't in, I drove round a bit. (*Pause.*) Drove down to the old house. By the canal. (*Pause.*) Doesn't look much different. A bloody dog rushed out and sank its teeth into me trouser leg. (*Pause.*) What? Oh, yes. Better than bullet holes. Aye. (*Pause.*) You're looking pretty fit. (*Long pause.*) That's not sciatica. It's all that bloody gardening. Your spine must be like a DNA molecule. (*Pause.*) Of *course* I don't expect you to know what I'm talking about. It's just a weak form of aggression, dad. Me displaying my cultural superiority. Or something. (*Long pause.*) She what? Fell off the hen-house roof? What was the old bugger doing *on* the hen-house roof? She must be eighty-three if she's a day. Knowing her, I'd say she was up there with the binoculars. (*Pause.*) Broken hip? I expect they'll give her an aluminium ball-and-socket. (*Long pause.*) I just thought I'd drop in. I'm lecturing in Harrogate tomorrow. (*Pause.*) Yes. I know. (*Pause.*) Harrogate ought to be shitten on by a fleet of airborne rhinoceri. (*Long pause.*) I was in the Soviet Union last week. (*Long pause.*) Dad – how can you make the long and tortuous jump from the Soviet Union to me Cousin Donald in two sentences? (*Pause.*) Well, he's getting on then, isn't he? Cousin Donald. Climbing up. Yes. (*Pause.*) Got all his *degrees* for Customs Officer, has he? Well, that's grand. Fine. Let's hope they post him to London Airport. I'm always having scenes there. (*Pause.*) He was an awful little bastard. Used to sit in the woods of a summer's day catching flies with his foreskin. (*Pause.*) By God, you don't half go granite-faced when I say something blue. (*Pause.*) Now I know why it is I'm an intellectual bigot. Me mother had all the so-called 'native' intelligence and you had all the dumb prejudice. (*Pause.*) You're as thick as a post. (*Long pause.*) Been mulling over the Twentieth Party Congress, have you? (*Pause.*)

Of *course* I didn't bloody think you had. (*Long pause.*) I have
scenes at London Airport because I have this tendency to
arrive there drunk, you know. From here and there. Coming and
going. Globe-trotting Bernard. (*Pause.*) I can't wait to see me
Cousin Donald's face should we confront each other on the
official level, so to speak, one day. (*Pause.*) They're all sadists,
but wait till they get him in the ranks. (*Pause.*) Nepotism is a
word that's probably not in Donald's vocabulary. But if it is,
he won't shove much of it my way. Not at London Airport he
won't. (*Pause.*) Dad. What's more interesting about that pig-
nosed little turd becoming a Customs Officer than me going to
the Soviet Union? I ask you that in your full capacity as a
working man. (*Long pause.*) Dad, I *don't* hate you. I really don't.
It's just that since me mother died I've begun to *register* you in a
different way. That's all.

    Fade out and fade in to

Scene Five

BERNARD'S *room as before, but* CHRIS *is preparing to build some
shelves. He is planing a long plank on two wooden trestles. It is night.
A single bright standard lamp sheds light where* CHRIS *is working.*
CLAIRE *is sewing. We hear a distant train, the howl of an ambulance.
A long silence. The gentle swish of the plane along the wood.*

CLAIRE. You're working late, Chris.

CHRIS. Working? It's a bloody holiday when Rodge isn't here.
    Wriggling his arse. Cooing. (*Pause.*) See where there's all white
    paint spattered on the parquet? That's Rodge. (*Pause.*) Ber-
    nard's all right, though. Take these shelves. Well, it isn't part of
    the job, see. But Bernard, he'll ask you to do a bit extra and
    stick a tenner in your fist as well as pay for the job. (*Pause.*)
    And I don't screw him, neither. I take the bread. I do him a
    good job. (*Pause.*) How's the kid?

CLAIRE. Oh, he's O.K.

Pause.

CHRIS. I wouldn't have thought sewing was in your line.

CLAIRE. I'm not sewing. What my hands are doing, it's a kind of mini-wrestling. The result will be grotesque. (*Pause.*) You should grasp the idea that ineptitude has its uses in life.

CHRIS. I don't get you.

CLAIRE. I mean this: my mental picture of walking the kid out, you know. In his carriage. My vision is that he should look like he was a demented Lap. The son of a demented Lap. The grandchild of a demented Lap. And so on, backwards into the dark mists of ancestral time.

Pause.

CHRIS. I thought you was rich –

CLAIRE. There is no contradiction between the possession of money and the desire for your kid to look like something the reindeer brought in.

Pause.

CHRIS. He'll have to move down here, when we're doing his room.

Pause.

CLAIRE. Rass?

CHRIS. No, I mean Bernard. (*Pause.*) Or *you* will and he can have yours. (*Pause.*) Then we shall be doing yours, and –

CLAIRE. You think *I* should get on to some goddam truckle bed down here whilst he –

CHRIS. It isn't what I think. It's just you'll have to work it out between the two of you. (*Pause.*) If you're staying.

CLAIRE. Listen. I'm taking advantage of Bernard whilst I've got him. It's no secret. So I'm rich and I could stay in a hotel. Or anywhere. But here's where I lived with Haggerty and here's where I stay for a while. Till I've carried out a few investigations. Like, if Bernard was *capable* of getting me out I'd be out. Wouldn't I? There'd be no problem.

Pause.

CHRIS. You hurt Bernard.

Pause.

CLAIRE. So I hurt Bernard. That's like saying I breathe! If he put his boot in my can I'd whizz out like any other sonofabitch. Bam! Down the stairs. Rass dangling from my nerveless fingers. (*Pause.*) *Could* he dangle though? With *that* amount of hair? You seen Rass's hair? What nature proposes turpentine disposes?

> CHRIS *has finished the plank, taken it off the trestle, and now he leans it against the wall. He takes a broom and begins to sweep up the wood-shavings.*

CHRIS. I wish you'd lay off Rodge, as well.

CLAIRE. Lay *off* Roger? I'm the first time the concepts 'lay' and 'female' have been brought together in the poor little bastard's life!

> *Pause.*

CHRIS. He's not bad. Underneath. (*Pause.*) *I* needle him all day as well.

> *Pause.*

CLAIRE. Chris, you choke me. I mean, you really do.

> *Pause.*

CHRIS. Let it drop about the turps. That's all. (*Pause.*) Then Rodge won't rib you so much either. (*Pause.*) He's like that.

CLAIRE. Thank God he isn't American! Think what the little twink could do with *napalm*!

> *Pause.*

CHRIS. Bernard's very good with Rodge.

> *Pause.*

CLAIRE. OK. So the scalp defoliation incident shall never more be referred to. I submit. You raped me into a state of grace.

> *Pause.*

CHRIS. Bernard tell you I knew Haggerty?

CLAIRE. Yeah. (*Pause.*) Haggerty in depth? Or just once-a-week-therapy?

> *Pause.*

CHRIS. For about half an hour. (*Pause.*) I once came here to – see,

I was working for a builder's then. We was rung up and Haggerty said he had this roof fallen in.

CLAIRE. Which roof?

CHRIS. Well, it's Rass's, now.

> *Pause.*

CLAIRE. If only the man himself had been underneath it!

> *Pause.*

CHRIS. So me and my mate, we come round to have a look at the damage. Sort of estimate it. (*Pause.*) And when he answered the door, your husband's crying.

CLAIRE. Haggerty *crying*?

CHRIS. You could tell he'd *been* crying. From his face –

CLAIRE. I didn't assume even he would greet you with his ass! Though it's not entirely out of the question.

CHRIS. Mrs Haggerty –

CLAIRE. You think I was *married* to him?

> *Pause.*

CHRIS. That's none of my business. I mean, what you and he was in your relationship, and –

CLAIRE. It wasn't a relationship. It was a labyrinth.

> *Pause.*

CHRIS. Frank and me. We have a look at the ceiling, and that. Then your . . . Haggerty brings out the drinks and we have a chat and we tell him the score with the ceiling. And we leave. (*Pause.*) I never did the ceiling meself. I was bloody fed up with my firm anyway. So I starts this with Rely-On.

> *Pause.*

CLAIRE. And so what was it about Haggerty? That hit you so hard? In your guts. In half an hour.

> *Pause.*
>
> CHRIS *has the shavings in a neat pile. With a brush and pan, he gathers them in.*

Shall we talk about something else? I can be garrulous on a fantastic variety of subjects.

> *Pause.*

CHRIS. Ask yourself. What was you to Haggerty? And him to you? (*Pause.*) When you split up. (*Pause.*) Why. (*Pause.*) All that. (*Pause.*) It's time I was off.

CLAIRE. You got a bird?

CHRIS. Not just now.

> *Pause.*

CLAIRE. Live with your parents?

CHRIS. No. I've got a room. Paddington way.

> *He empties the shavings into a large, empty paint tin.* BERNARD *enters, looking tired. He is wearing an old short raincoat, open. He takes a notebook from the pocket and throws it down on his desk.*

CLAIRE. Hi –

CHRIS. I was just going, Bernard.

BERNARD (*notes the beginning of the shelves*). You shouldn't have stayed so late.

CHRIS. No odds to me.

CLAIRE. A drink?

BERNARD. Yes. I'd like one. Why don't you have one before you go, Chris?

CHRIS. Thanks.

> CLAIRE *goes into the kitchen.* BERNARD *sinks into a chair, rubbing his face with his hands. He takes out a packet of cigarettes, offers one to* CHRIS, *who shakes his head, and lights one for himself.*

Been at the theatre?

BERNARD. Yes.

CHRIS. Crap?

BERNARD. Crap.

> *Pause.*

CHRIS. It'd drive me up the wall.

BERNARD (*points up at the ceiling*). That's exactly where I am.

> CHRIS *looks towards the kitchen, then back at* BERNARD. *Pulls a telegram from his trouser pocket.*

CHRIS. This come this afternoon.

BERNARD. Why the secrecy? (*He takes it, opens it.*)

CHRIS. It's International.

BERNARD (*just beginning to read*). So?

CHRIS. I sort of thought it might be from Him.

BERNARD. Do I hear a capital 'H' on the Him? As, for example, when referring to some deity?

　　Pause.

CHRIS. But it is, though. Isn't it?

BERNARD. Correct.

　　Pause.

CHRIS. None of my business.

BERNARD. I get your drift entirely. Therefore listen. It says: WHEN BITCH ARRIVES WILL BE VIOLENT AND EXPLOIT YOU STOP. DISSIMULATE SUBMISSION STOP. REMEMBER J. JOYCE: SILENCE, EXILE AND CUNNING STOP. HAGGERTY.

　　CLAIRE *enters with a tray: ice, whisky, glasses. As she comes in,* BERNARD *stuffs the telegram in his pocket. She puts the tray on the desk. Pours three drinks. Gives one each to* BERNARD *and* CHRIS. *Takes one herself.*

　　BERNARD *and* CHRIS *sip their drinks in silence.*

CLAIRE. You need a new ice-box.

BERNARD. I know.

　　There is a long silence. CLAIRE *looks from* CHRIS *to* BERNARD.

CLAIRE. What's with what?

　　Pause.

BERNARD. Nothing.

　　CHRIS *finishes his drink quickly and makes for the door.*

CHRIS. Time I was off. See you tomorrow.

BERNARD. 'Night, Chris –

CLAIRE (*as the door closes*). G'night, Chris –

　　She moves to a chair and sits with her drink. BERNARD *takes off his raincoat and goes with his drink to the typewriter.*

　　You writing your piece tonight?

BERNARD (*looking at his notebook*). Yes.

Pause.

CLAIRE. I guess I'll just finish my drink.

BERNARD. What time does Rass get *his* drink?

Pause.

CLAIRE. You know, when I came in just now –

BERNARD. Yes?

CLAIRE. With the drinks –

BERNARD. Yes?

CLAIRE. There was an 'atmosphere'. Between you and Chris. A real atmosphere.

BERNARD. Oh, I don't think so.

CLAIRE. Digging round for a good word for the atmosphere. I'd say it was *palpable*.

Pause.

BERNARD. D'you know what tonight's play was like?

CLAIRE. What?

BERNARD. I really mean – what it *was*.

CLAIRE. What was it?

BERNARD. A third-rate misfiring farce, written by an unconscious reactionary who thinks he's a combination of Strindberg and Lenin.

Pause.

CLAIRE. Well, at least –

BERNARD. At least what?

CLAIRE. You got the opening blast of your review in one sentence.

Pause.

BERNARD. I think I probably have.

Pause.

CLAIRE. Type away, Bernard. Ignore me. I need a couple of drinks, though.

Pause.

BERNARD. I always hate this bit. (*Pause.*) When I've got in. And it's late. And quiet. And I've got to commit myself to a few paragraphs.

Pause.

CLAIRE. Don't you ever see either of your wives? Or ex-mistresses? Or mistress or something, dammit?

BERNARD. First wife won't see me. Hasn't for ten years. (*Pause.*) I ring her once a year. Husband answers. (*Pause.*) When it's only once a year – why do I always get *him*?

CLAIRE. I'd say the problem defies statistical analysis.
   Pause.

BERNARD. And my second wife. Is in Australia. (*Pause.*) Lives with a professor of philosophy.

CLAIRE. They have philosophy in *Australia*?

BERNARD. Must have. (*Pause.*) I expect they have it everywhere. In one way or another.

CLAIRE. Yeah. I expect he wrote a brilliant thesis for his doctorate entitled: Baaaaaaaaa.
   Pause.

BERNARD. She owes me a hundred pounds. (*Pause.*) Left, owing me a hundred. (*Pause.*) That was their first two months' rent when they shacked up together in London.
   Pause.

CLAIRE. You miss the hundred?
   Pause.

BERNARD. No. But before he got the job in Australia, I used to think. Used to imagine them in their flat. In their bedroom. (*Pause.*) Banging away. (*Pause.*) And I'd hear myself suddenly yell, as I reflected: AND IT'S MY BLOODY HUNDRED. (*Pause.*) Once I was very pissed about three in the morning and I rang them to shout down the phone: IT'S MY BLOODY HUNDRED.
   Pause.

CLAIRE. What happened?

BERNARD. Well, *he* answered. He was rather forthright, considering who owed whom and how much. He said: Get stuffed – *bourgeois*!

CLAIRE. And you said?

BERNARD. He rang off. I fell asleep.

CLAIRE. Bernard. I think you better work. And I'll just sit here and be quiet. Or I shall start tearing you limb from limb.
> *Pause.*

BERNARD. I know what you mean. But you see apart from the question of guilt. Of which I think he was incapable. He *did* have some cause for resentment.

CLAIRE. Being?

BERNARD. I paid them for their abortion. Her abortion. Just after she left me.

CLAIRE. Jesus Christ almighty!
> *Pause.*

BERNARD. That was another hundred.
> *Pause.*

CLAIRE. I can see you really brutalized this guy!

BERNARD. Yes. That's what I mean.

CLAIRE. *Mean* is the word. *Mean*-escalating-to-*sadistic*. (*Pause.*) You wicked Link!

BERNARD. I know. That's why the second hundred comes in a special category. Sort of psychic equivalent of tax-relief. I call it: THE AGGRESSIVE HUNDRED. (*Pause.*) Sounds like one of those Crimean Battles. Doesn't it?

CLAIRE. I gather you don't crave for the second hundred then?

BERNARD. No. That was money well spent. (*Pause.*) Only the first hundred. (*Pause.*) I'm not only bourgeois. I'm liberal, with it. (*Pause.*) And secretly, turbulent with hatred. (*Pause.*) Ho ho.

CLAIRE. We better not send you to my place in Amagansett. (*Pause.*) I think definitely not.
> *There is a long silence. Then* BERNARD *switches on his desk lamp and begins to type.* CLAIRE *sits with her glass held to her lips.*
> *Fade out and fade in to*

Scene Six

The stage is dark. An illuminated sign is lowered saying: HAVANA. *A single spot picks out* BERNARD *standing in his shirt sleeves. A second spot picks out an* INTERPRETER *standing just behind him, left.*

BERNARD. The delegate from the United Arabic Republic said – I believe I quote him correctly – 'If we are to take bread from the people to buy a spotlight in a theatre: then the people must have some control over what happens beneath that spotlight.' I wish to propose a special discussion of the implications of that statement.

The INTERPRETER *steps forward and repeats what he has said in Spanish.*

The spots on BERNARD *and the* INTERPRETER *fade as he continues.*

I am aware that the Assembly may consider this proposal an unwelcome digression from the actual contents of today's agenda. None the less –

Fade out spots on BERNARD *and* INTERPRETER. *Darkness whilst* BERNARD *puts on a jacket.*

Fade up BERNARD *pulling forward a chair and sitting down to face the audience.*

Dad – who can resist you? Who can resist a man who writes: 'Your Uncle Charlie's had his other leg off. A finer man never wore a pair of boots'? (*Pause.*) Look, I'm only trying to say the statement has its comic side. (*Pause.*) I *know* there's nothing funny about losing both your legs. For God's sake! (*Pause.*) Look. I was in the bloody blasted war, you know! (*Pause.*) What? (*Pause.*) I've told you before. I got that wound in the arse when I was climbing out of a burning tank! It's not, cowardice-wise, a question of which way I was pointing, dad. (*Pause.*) How could I be running away from the Germans when the sods had us encircled? Go on! Tell me! And tell me, whilst we're at it, why you have to bring it up about three times a year? (*Pause.*) You've given me more scars talking about it than the actual piece of bloody shrapnel! (*Pause.*) I *know* it's not the same as Uncle Charlie. So he gets one chopped off down the pit, and one sawn off years later in hospital. I mean, I suppose the surgeon knew what he was doing. I just – (*Long pause.*) All right. I'll accept that. We'll try to stay off 'controversial topics'. Jesus. (*Long pause.*) Dad, you don't believe in God either so why get worked up about me saying Jesus? (*Long pause.*) Yes. I expect I am a bit tanned. I've been in Cuba. I wrote and told you I was *going*. All I can say is your memory for anything to do with me has *gone*. It simply doesn't function. (*Long pause.*) Well, I was a bit frightened of sharks. Sea's boiling with sharks round there. *And* barracuda. (*Long pause.*) Three and a half pounds, was it? A perch? Down at Crawston Dam. (*Pause.*) Dad. Don't say things like: 'From the sublime to the ridiculous'! Please. There is *no* contest on between my sharks and your perch. None whatsoever. (*Long pause.*) What? You thought Cuba was part of America and it's been and gone and gone communist?

BERNARD *stands, looking in front of him woodenly. Long pause.* Dad. Your mind doesn't have ideas. It has enigmatically related confusions. (*Pause.*) Sorry. (*Pause.*) I was about to say there *was* a sense in which Cuba was part of the USA. But it bloody well isn't any more! (*Long pause.*) Why are you crying? (*Pause.*) All my life I thought you were something like a mute. (*Pause.*) *She* did all the talking. (*Pause.*) Now *you* do the talking. (*Pause.*) And when you revert. When you go mute. Which is to say: when I begin to think I recognize you again – dammit, you cry! (*Long pause.*) Padre o muerte! Venceremos!

Fade out and fade in to

Scene Seven

The same as Scene 5, but later in the small hours. The room is dark, lit only by a street lamp outside. CLAIRE *is asleep in her chair.* BERNARD *enters from the upstairs exit. He stands watching her a moment. Then he goes to her and gently shakes her.*

BERNARD. Claire –

She is instantly awake, reaching beside her for her glass. BERNARD *goes to the desk and switches on the lamp, pulling it down so that the room is only softly lit.*

CLAIRE. What time is it?

BERNARD. Just after four.

CLAIRE. Oh, my God! The kid –

BERNARD. It's all right. He started howling. I went up and fed him and he went back to sleep.

She rubs her face with her hands.

CLAIRE. Seems like I drank the whole damn bottle.

BERNARD. Most of it.

CLAIRE. You manage to finish your piece?

BERNARD. Yes.

CLAIRE. I hope it was a good old stinger-roo.

BERNARD. The tone was one of stylish malice.

Pause.

CLAIRE. I'm sorry about the kid.

BERNARD *goes to the desk and gets his glass. He pours a drink from the whisky bottle beside* CLAIRE'S *chair.*

BERNARD. How d'you feel?

Pause.

CLAIRE. Muzzy. And vicious.

Pause.

BERNARD. I'll just have one drink. Then I'll get out of the firing line.

CLAIRE. I mean generalized vicious, Bernard. Not you.

C

Pause.

BERNARD. Long time since I mixed and administered a feed.

CLAIRE. You take a good look at him?

BERNARD. Not much point in looking elsewhere. What with having the teat rammed into his little mouth. And the trickling, and so on.

Pause.

CLAIRE. Cross your mind he looks like Mao Tse Tung?

BERNARD. Looks like any baby. To my mind they always do. (*Pause.*) Shouldn't you get some sleep?

CLAIRE. I just had some, didn't I?

BERNARD. In bed, I meant.

CLAIRE. Sleep is sleep.

Pause.

BERNARD. Aren't you a bit pissed, though?

CLAIRE. My mouth tastes like a weasel's foreskin. Otherwise – compos mentis.

BERNARD *sits opposite her.*

BERNARD. I'm a bit of an insomniac. Usually about this time I have a few last drinks and play some nostalgic record or other.

Pause.

CLAIRE. Times of love.

BERNARD. I expect so. Yes. Records are better than milestones. What with them being round and flat. And when you stick a needle on them they induce sensations. Which can be carefully regulated according to mood. (*Pause.*) It's my favourite time. In one eye a tear, in the other a glint. When I think of my lacerating comments on the theatre of this-that-or-the-other. (*Pause.*) A harmless form of omnipotence.

CLAIRE. Except for the poor sod who wrote the play.

Pause.

BERNARD. Most of the best playwrights don't give a damn about the notices. Quite rightly, I and my fellow criticism-grubbers are simply unreal to them. (*Pause.*) I like that, since the notion that I am unreal coincides with my own self-evaluations.

(*Pause.*) Also, I might add. If it's a good play – I give it a thorough analysis and unstinting praise. Needless to say, that is a rare enough strain on my feeble reserves of generosity. (*Pause.*) All these things combined, well . . . they concede me a certain grudging respect.

He drinks. CLARE *takes a small drink.*

CLAIRE. You going to play one of your milestones, then?

Pause.

BERNARD. I think: a touch of the Leonard Cohen's. But this one, I assure you, is emotionally neutral. (*Pause.*) Partly because I discover these singers about two years after everyone's been at them for at least a year. (*Pause.*) And the last year has been . . . from the woman point of view, shall we say? Pretty arid.

As BERNARD *goes to the Hi-Fi, which is a jumble of gear on the floor in one corner :*

CLAIRE. I *told* you. The idea of laying me *did* flicker across your – dare I say it after so much unjust irony? – across your mind?

BERNARD *starts the Leonard Cohen record. Resumes his seat.*

BERNARD. Must get a new typewriter. It seemed to make an awful clatter when you were sitting there asleep behind me.

CLAIRE. And a new ice-box.

BERNARD. We've already agreed that.

Pause.

CLAIRE. That's Haggerty's ice-box.

Pause.

BERNARD. He left a few things.

Pause.

CLAIRE. Haggerty was always unlucky with artefacts. Anything man-made: walls, floors, windows, electronic stuff. You know what I mean? You had the impression when Haggerty moved in somewhere, the gadgetry of civilization went on strike. He is the only man I know who actually did get his penis trapped by the lid on the lavatory bowl. (*Pause.*) For example. The lid was in the up position one moment, as for standard male-usage. The

next it was pinning his poor old prick to the porcelain. (*Pause.*)
It was like he took poltergeists with him. Everywhere.

BERNARD. If we take your description as correct, he must have
been something of an acrobat.

CLAIRE. Use your head, Bernard! He was kneeling. He had it
over the goddam side of the bowl.

BERNARD. Kneeling to pee? Was he a kind of micturitional
evangelist?

CLAIRE. Haggerty was often drunk. And when in the john liked
to keep his head low in case he should throw up.

  BERNARD *reflects, drinking.*

BERNARD. Then he must quite often have been belted across the
head by the lavatory lid. (*Pause.*) Therefore, I suppose on the
occasion you describe, he was also leaning backwards? His head
backwards? (*Pause.*) Or else the genital would never have been
struck. (*Pause.*) I think.

  Pause.

CLAIRE. I never worked it out, Bernard. I haven't got the academic twist of mind, like you.

  Pause.

BERNARD. Talking of academic matters. I'm lecturing in Paris
tomorrow evening. To some of those students, you know? Who
are a trifle iconoclastic these days. About art.

CLAIRE. They'll pull your guts out and hang them over the
Sorbonne.

  Pause.

BERNARD. Curious. At forty-five, one has to face the fact that one
is a mere relic. (*Pause.*) Culturally, a relic.

CLAIRE. There are plenty of guys facing that problem in New
York at thirty!

  Pause.

BERNARD. Do you like the Leonard Cohen, Claire?

CLAIRE. I don't like any kind of music. Especially emotional mile-
stone music.

BERNARD. Which I said it wasn't.

CLAIRE (*rising*). I'm going up. You finish your drink and enjoy what you enjoy, Bernard. Rass's id – I think they only have id at this stage, don't they? His id will be in full voice between six and seven. (*Pause.*) What time's your plane?

BERNARD. About one p.m. Air France. I always go Air France, Orly being nearer the city than Le Bour –

CLAIRE (*cutting in*). Sleep late and I'll call you around eleven. OK?

BERNARD. Fine.

She goes to the door. At the door, turning:

CLAIRE. The Mormons were here this morning.

BERNARD. *What?*

CLAIRE. Yeah. Mormons. At your door. My door. Haggerty's door. You know? Mormons?

BERNARD. I know what they *are*.

CLAIRE. They looked like they were fresh out of some CIA training establishment. Mormons, I said? Don't give me that, fellers. You get back to the good old USA and piss into the files. That, I said, might guarantee you a place beside the Lord.

BERNARD. Oh dear.

CLAIRE. Why oh dear?

Pause.

BERNARD. It's just . . . I've had a certain amount of attention from the Special Branch. In my time. Here in London. And –

CLAIRE. Don't lose your cool, Bernard. I told them I was your cleaning woman and you're a Roman Catholic. I figured it this way: Mormons or CIA, how will they push *this* conversation?

BERNARD. And how did they?

CLAIRE. They bowed their nice all-American cropped heads and withdrew. For your further edification, quite by accident I had a long sharp carving knife in my hand. Carving knife, huh? You *do* remember we had roast lamb for lunch?

BERNARD (*distractedly*). Oh, yes. Very nice it was. Yes. Roast lamb. (*Pause.*) And string beans.

CLAIRE. I warn you, Bernard. From now on it's out with the carbohydrates and in with the proteins. Huh?

BERNARD *is still abstracted, but looks down at his paunch.*

BERNARD. It never works, you know. Not with me.

CLAIRE. I'm gonna starve that paunch to within an inch of its life. (*Pause.*) Before I go.

BERNARD. I see.

CLAIRE. So you either collaborate. Or you've got me for an even longer stretch than you had in mind.

Pause.

BERNARD. Starvation it is, then!

CLAIRE. G'night, Bernard –

BERNARD. Good night, Claire.

She goes out. BERNARD *goes to the record and changes it. He goes back to his chair and his drink. Softly, a Mozart* BASSOON CONCERTO *wells up.* BERNARD *goes and switches off the desk light. Returns to his seat – once more the room is lit by the street lamp.*

Fade out and fade in to

Scene Eight

The stage is dark. An illuminated sign is lowered saying : PRAGUE. *A spot picks out* BERNARD, *in his jacket. A second spot picks out an* INTERPRETER *standing just behind him, left.*

Above and behind them, suspended, there is the effect of a human figure slowly burning. This continues throughout.

BERNARD. I can hardly speak.

The INTERPRETER *translates this immediately in Czech.*

(*More aloofly and formally.*) You know. And I know. That it is impossible for me to give the proposed lecture on contemporary English Drama. Or for you to listen.

The INTERPRETER *translates this.*

I have no doubt that many of you . . . share . . . my disgust . . .

with the hypocritical indignation of the Western countries. (*Pause.*) Even in your anguish. (*Pause.*) Your isolation. (*Pause.*) Someone said to me yesterday: don't come here from your comfortable house in London to tell us what a Marxist you are. (*Pause.*) I had no such intention, of course. (*Pause.*) There are many ways of burning. (*Pause.*) But let each way, each fire, consume whatever is destroying our humanity. (*Pause.*) I can say no more.

> BERNARD *stands expressionless, whilst the* INTERPRETER *translates in Czech. As she finishes, a slow clapping begins. The* INTERPRETER *comes forward, her back to the audience, facing* BERNARD. *She takes up the clapping rhythm herself. This continues for a few seconds.*
>
> *The spots on* BERNARD *and the* INTERPRETER *fade. The clapping stops. The burning human figure fades into darkness. Darkness for a few seconds.*
>
> *Fade up* BERNARD *pulling forward a chair. He sits. There is a long pause.*

I see. (*Pause.*) You were ill. You were alone. Nobody came to see you. Nobody even popped in and offered to do you a bit of shopping. (*Pause.*) Mrs Lambert next door's what? Been taken into mental hospital? (*Long pause: he stands pointing.*) The bloody telephone's still there, isn't it? (*He sits.*) Why did I . . . ? (*His voice fades away wearily.*) Why do you think I had the sodding phone put *in*? (*Long pause.*) I see. I should have telephoned *you*, dad. (*Long pause.*) I'm telepathic. I'm clairvoyant. I *know* you're ill without being told. Eh? (*Pause.*) Oh. (*Pause.*) Yes, I see. When I was in Jugoslavia. But it was Czechoslovakia. (*Pause.*) That's right. (*Pause.*) So why didn't you ring the doctor? The Old People's Welfare? Downing Street? (*Long pause.*) Dad, I only use sarcasm to your actual face because I can usually rely on it not penetrating your skull. And that is therapeutic. Yes, for me, I mean. It normally relieves my tensions without damaging *you*. (*Long pause.*) What? It was Mr Lambert's sarcasm sent Mrs Lambert round the bend? (*Pause.*)

You and I have conflicting views on mental illness, dad. (*Long pause.*) Yes. I know. On everything. (*Long pause.*) I feel like getting down on my knees and pleading your forgiveness for not being a Customs Officer. (*Pause.*) Your scale of what constitutes human achievement is one I comprehend – but reject. See? What's more, I roll in from Prague and me Cousin Donald *is* at London Airport. What does he do? Carves me up for having three bottles of slivotiz instead of one. You should have seen the smarmy expression on his face. I said – I was high, I'll admit – I said: Donald, let me take the two offending bottles and pour them down the lav. What did he say? By all means, he said. But you'll still have to pay the tax because you brought them *in*. (*Pause.*) I turned to his – what do they call it? Colleague? And yelled: that man used to catch flies under his – (*Pause.*) OK, OK, I'll wash me dirty mouth out. (*Pause.*) Dad I am forty-five. (*Pause.*) Drink? What's drinking got to do with it? (*Pause.*) You're ashamed to have me Cousin Donald see me pissed at the airport? I am ashamed of your shame.

Fade out and fade in to

Scene Nine

As the previous night, except the drinks have been cleared and the typewriter is covered. It is afternoon.

An old man enters – at least, he is over seventy. A big man in an old but well-brushed and pressed suit, a checked shirt with a large bulging knot on his tie, and a trilby hat. He carries a brown paper carrier.

He looks round : the room is empty. He takes off his raincoat, folds it and puts it over a chair back. He removes his hat and places it carefully on the desk.

He sits in the middle of the room, his back straight, his hands on his knees. Physically, he is a formidable size and shape. He looks awkward but dignified.

ROGER *enters, wearing denim shirt and trousers, and a flowered kerchief. He is carrying a large paint tin. Looks wretched. The old man – BERNARD'S FATHER – has his back to the hall door and doesn't turn. ROGER crosses the room and into the kitchen with the paint tin. The FATHER takes out a flat tin of tobacco, papers, and begins to roll a cigarette.*

ROGER *comes a few steps out of the kitchen.*

ROGER. Hello.

FATHER. How d'ye do.

Pause.

ROGER. It's . . . er . . . I think it's in the kitchen. Under the sink.

Pause.

FATHER. What is?

ROGER. The (*failing*) – the meter. Mmmm?

FATHER. Well, I'm very interested to hear that. I always like to know where t'meter is.

Pause.

ROGER. Not Gas Board? London Electricity?

FATHER *looks up from rolling his cigarette.*

FATHER. Young man. I bought this suit off t'peg in Doncaster in nineteen fifty-two. (*Pause.*) Now. To you it might very well make me look like t'gas man. To me it were a bloody bargain.

ROGER *hovers, as always wary of instantaneous attack.*

ROGER. Then –?

FATHER. Then I had Mother take up t'cuffs an inch. And after that it were champion. (*Holds one arm out.*) Feel that material.

ROGER. Might one ask how you got *in*?

FATHER. One might. One found t'door open. (*Pause.*) And while we're about it. Might *one* ask you who the bloody hell you are?

ROGER (*pertly*). I was going to ask you the very same thing!

Pause.

FATHER. I'm Mister Link's father

Pause.

ROGER. *Oh*, dear me! I *am* sorry!

FATHER. Don't let it put thy nose out of joint.

ROGER. Terrible brick dropper! I'm *awful*.

> *Pause.*

FATHER. Be that as it may.

> *Pause.*

ROGER. You see, Bernard's in Paris. Doing his talkie-talkie bit.

FATHER. Eh?

ROGER. He's giving a lecture in Paris. Would you like a cup of
tea?

FATHER. I wouldn't say no. I've just come off t'train.

ROGER. Was it ghastly? From where was it?

FATHER. You wouldn't know it. Little place near Doncaster.
Heard of Doncaster, 'ave you?

ROGER. Look, I'm devastated, you know? With shame? I mean
about the Gas Board.

FATHER. Nay, lad. Sometimes when I go into a pub in Doncaster,
they take me for a detective. What does't think on that? Eh?

ROGER. I don't really know, Mr Link.

FATHER. It's me feet, tha sees. An' me raincoat. And t'way I *hold*
meself, if you get me. I *hold* meself like a detective. I've been
told so. (*Pause : he chuckles.*) I've seen some faces drop when I've
gone in one or two places after closin' time. (*Pause.*) Our Bernard, he – are you a friend on his, then?

> *Pause.*

ROGER. Well, not exactly a friend –

FATHER. Not from t'Gas Board, are you?

> ROGER *greets this with a sickly smile.*

I like a feller as can take a joke.

ROGER (*muted*). I'm in this firm that's doing his flat up. Rely-On.

FATHER. *Rely-On*, is it? Now there's a name for a firm. Somebody's got their head on their shoulders.

ROGER. Yes. Well. It isn't me. I'm just one of their wretched serfs.

FATHER. Serfs? I thought them was abolished in the nineteenth
century. (*Pause.*) Tolstoy's time, round about. Wasn't it?

Pause.

ROGER. It was a manner of speaking, Mr Link.

FATHER. Nay, I've read a thing or two about serfs. In me time.
Mind you. I'm only a self-educated man, Mr –

ROGER. Call me Roger.

FATHER. Call you anything you like, lad. But between you and
me. I haven't read a book for nigh twenty years. Haven't found
one that caught me interest, you know. (*Pause.*) When's he
due back, then?

ROGER. Well, you never know. With Bernard.

Pause.

FATHER. I'll give you that one! Straight away.

ROGER. I mean. *Quite* a will-o'-the-wisp! Isn't he?

FATHER. I'll tell thee what, lad.

ROGER. What?

FATHER. I'm gagging for that cup o' tea. I don't want to trouble
you. I'd get it meself. Only I've never been here before.

ROGER. Milk and shug?

FATHER. If it's no trouble.

> ROGER *starts for the kitchen, then comes back to the* FATHER
> *confidingly.* MR LINK *sits, as always, with his hands on his
> knees.*

ROGER. Er –

FATHER. Go on, lad. Go on!

ROGER. I don't know whether I ought to say. *Warn,* I was *going*
to say –

Pause.

FATHER. What's up?

Pause.

ROGER. 'Course, the place is in an awful mess to start with. But
apart from that. (*Pause: semi-whisper.*) There's an L-A-D-Y
living here. (*Pause.*) If that's the word for her.

FATHER. Eh, that's nowt new! He's 'ad more than one companion
since his last divorce. Does't think I'm narrow minded or sum-
at?

ROGER. She's got a baby as well.

   Pause.

FATHER. Oh, aye? That *will* take a minute to sink in, I'll admit.
   First he's had out of wedlock as far as I know.

   Pause.

ROGER. Oh, it's not *Bernard's*, Mr Link! Oh dear me, no!

   CLAIRE *enters with a polythene bag crammed with laundry,*
   from the door leading upstairs.

CLAIRE. Roger, I –

   She stops and registers the scene. MR LINK *sits impassively.*

   (*sharply to* ROGER.) I was about to say I shall be at the laund-
   erette for the next half-hour. I thought Chris might keep an eye
   on Rass.

ROGER. Mr Link. This is the lady I was telling you about. Claire
   dear, Bernard's father. All the way from Doncaster.

   MR LINK *gets up and holds his hand out.* CLAIRE *drops the bag*
   and shakes hands with him.

FATHER. How d'you do, love –

CLAIRE. Glad to meet you, Mr Link. And surprised too, because
   Bernard's –

FATHER. In Paris. Aye. T'young man told me. (*Pause.*) If I've
   caught you at an inconvenient moment –

ROGER. I was just going to make a cuppa –

   ROGER *flits off into the kitchen.* MR LINK *sits down.*

FATHER. I hope I'm not putting nobody about –

CLAIRE. Of course you aren't. Only, I'm sure Bernard wasn't
   expecting –

FATHER. Well, he wouldn't be, would he? I hadn't told him I was
   coming. When I were sitting in t'train: I thowt – wait till I see
   yon one's face. (*Pause.*) When you come to think about it, I'm
   bloody lucky if I see his face at *all*. (*Pause.*) Since his mother
   passed on. (*Pause.*) You know what our Bernard does?

CLAIRE. He never mentioned his parents.

FATHER. Aye. Well, tha sees, he's nobbut *one*. That's me.

CLAIRE. I'm sorry –

FATHER. Nay. Claire – can I call you Claire, is it?

CLAIRE. Sure.

FATHER. Are you his young lady?

Pause.

CLAIRE. I'm more a kind of visitor, Mr Link.

Pause.

FATHER. I take it you are from America. By the sound of your voice.

CLAIRE. That's right –

FATHER. I was going to say. What our Bernard does. He sends me ten quid a week to top up me pension. Then when it comes to setting *eyes* on him. Well, I can go and whistle, can't I? (*Pause.*) Not that he isn't a good lad. One of the best.

ROGER *enters with tea things on a tray. He sets it on a desk.*

ROGER. Can't we *phone* Bernard or something?

CLAIRE. Suppose you keep your cute little muzzle out of it, Roger?

ROGER (*mincing out*). See what I mean, Mr Link? Serf! And nothing in the Rely-On terms says we have to bend over hot kettles, either!

He exits.

FATHER. I say! That were a bit sharp, weren't it?

CLAIRE. Don't worry, Mr Link. If you went for Roger with a road drill it'd slide right off him.

Pause.

FATHER. I saw a programme about them on television.

CLAIRE. I beg your pardon?

FATHER. On telly. There's more about than you'd think. 'Omo-sexuals. Yer know? Omo. Like t'soap powder. Bit too much sex in them adverts, an' all. If you ask me. Which nobody does. Sex everywhere, it is. And as for *London* –

CLAIRE. Mr Link. Did you come down to see Bernard about any-thing special? Is it urgent, I mean?

Pause.

FATHER. Floods.

Pause.

CLAIRE. I'm sorry?

FATHER. Me house is flooded. Three feet o' water in t'back
  kitchen. And the way them houses is built, it isn't no bloody
  Noah's Ark neither. I can tell you. Talk about t'animals two be
  two! I'd like to march yon council into my *house* two be two.
  They'd need more than wellington boots. They'd need to be
  bloody frogmen.

  ROGER *comes busily in with the teapot. Set it down with the rest*
  of the things. Turns to CLAIRE.

ROGER. There we are, ducky. I won't say you be mum! We'd all
  be in fear of our lives, wouldn't we? So *I'll* pour.

CLAIRE. Where *is* Chris?

ROGER. Clearing up the shmatters in the back yard.

CLAIRE. You got a cup there for him?

ROGER. I have indeed. Chris has been very sunny of disposition
  today and has been awarded the Gnome. First class.

  ROGER *is pouring the tea.* FATHER *stares heavily at* CLAIRE.

FATHER. So there's two on them, is there?

ROGER. What's she been saying about me? (*Peering round.*)
  I don't see any luggage. Haven't you got any luggage, Mr
  Link?

FATHER. I have that.

ROGER. Must be invisible.

FATHER (*holds up his carrier*). It's in me carrier. Pyjamas. Two
  shirts. An' me razor. (*Pause.*) When Mother were alive, o'
  course, it were different. Two bloody big cases at least. Grand,
  staggering up and down them escilators on t'underground wi'
  two cases, eh? (*Pause.*) So now I always travel light, like.

  ROGER *gives him a cup of tea, and one to* CLAIRE. *He goes out*
  to the kitchen and we hear him calling:

ROGER (*off*), Chrissy! Chrissy!

  He comes back, as MR LINK *is clumsily holding his cup and*
  saucer and looking at the room.

FATHER. He's always shifting round, is our Bernard. Don't ask *me* what for. What were wrong wi' his last place? Up Hampstead. Now that had a reight bit o' garden, I put fifty daffodils on yon garden. (*Pause.*) He won't have brought them with him, I suppose?

ROGER *is peering archly at* CLAIRE *over the rim of his mug.*

ROGER. Seen Bernard's daffies anywhere?

FATHER. Nay, he'd not bother wi' flowers, wouldn't Bernard. Nature to him, it's either summat God made or his dad planted. And he doesn't give a bugger for neither on us.

ROGER. All we've got here's a weeny back yard, I'm afraid. Well, it's got three manky old trees and a border. Not much to get your teeth into, Mr Link. Chrissy – that's your other man from Rely-On. Chrissy's out there clearing it up a bit. I mean, we shoved all the empty paint tins and things out there.

CHRIS *enters, dirty and hot.* ROGER *immediately pours him his tea and offers him the Gnome.* CHRIS *stands looking at* MR LINK.

CLAIRE. Mr Link – Chris. Chris, this is Bernard's father.

FATHER. How d'ye do, Chris.

CHRIS (*comes forward and shakes* LINK'S *hand*). Pleased to meet you.

Long silence.

FATHER. I don't know why you three's got mugs an' I've got a cup and saucer. I never use a cup and saucer.

CLAIRE. Roger's a very refined person, Mr Link.

FATHER. Well, there's something in that. When *we* had visitors Mother always put out t'cups and saucers.

ROGER *puts his tongue out at* CLAIRE.

ROGER. See!

CHRIS (*to* ROGER). I thought you were going to paint that hall door –

ROGER. I *was*, sweetheart.

A long silence.

FATHER. Well. It's quite a bit on a tea party. Isn't it?

ROGER. Goodness knows *where* we're going to put you, Mr Link.

FATHER. Tha can peg me out on t'clothes line if tha likes, lad. I'm none fussy.

CHRIS (*sharply*). You get that paint, Rodge?

ROGER. Yes, I did! And for Bernard's room as well. *And* I got those hessian wallpaper samples he was talking about. (*Sniffs.*) Hessian! A bit camp for Bernard, don't you think?

  CHRIS *drains his mug and puts it down.*

CHRIS. Let's get on with it, then.

ROGER. I'm just going to take a couple of Disprins. I feel *awful*.

FATHER. I were just thinking. You don't look in very fine fettle. Not to me you don't.

  ROGER *goes to a mirror.* CHRIS, *with an angry expression, goes out.*

ROGER. It's my eyes. No?

FATHER. Aye. They look like summat staring out at you from a cat's backside. Don't they?

ROGER. *Charming!*

FATHER. Nay. Don't take on, lad.

  ROGER *turns from the mirror. He is crying.*

  Eh, lad. I didn't mean nowt. (*To* CLAIRE.) He's crying.

ROGER. It's not what you said, Mr Link. It's last night. A black man hit me. In Portobello Road.

FATHER. You want to watch out wi' them blackies.

ROGER. I do hope you aren't a racist, Mr Link.

FATHER. Where did he hit thee?

ROGER. On the ear. With his *knuckles*!

FATHER. Had tha done owt to offend him, then?

  Pause.

ROGER. I asked him for a light. That's all.

  Pause.

CLAIRE. For Jesus Christ's sake, Roger! Get the paint and start the hall door, will you? On the *hall* side.

  ROGER *glumly goes into the kitchen and emerges with a paint tin*

*and brush. Goes out through the hall door, casting a venomous
glance at* CLAIRE.

I guess it's all kind of bewildering, Mr Link. Would you like me
to explain?

FATHER. I don't want nobody to put theirselves about. Not for me
I don't. (*Pause.*) I can get t'evening train at King's Cross and
stop at his Auntie Bertha's, you know. *They* not flooded. They
live up by t'colliery. It's high ground, where they are.

CLAIRE. When did you last see Bernard?

FATHER. Oh, it'll be a bit, now. I don't know who invented family
ties; but any road, our Bernard must've come into t'world wi' a
pair of scissors. You know, to cut t'family ties?

CLAIRE. I'm right with you, Mr Link.

  Pause.

FATHER. It's funny how you can say things to a stranger.
(*Pause.*) Don't mind me calling you a stranger, love. I mean
nowt wrong by it. (*Pause.*) But I *do* get lonely. (*Pause.*) You'll
not know t'north of England, I suppose?

CLAIRE. I've been to Lincoln –

  Pause.

FATHER. Aye. Lincoln. You see, *that* – it's not exactly what *we*
call t'north. If you take me meaning. Up our way, we more like
call it t'south. (*Pause.*) That's if anybody were to bring it up,
like.

CLAIRE. Supposing you wash up, or whatever? And I'll kind of
put you in the Bernard picture –

FATHER (*startled*). Wash up?

  Pause.

CLAIRE. I meant: your hands? Or maybe you –

FATHER. My mistake love, *my* mistake. I assume you are using an
American expression. Wash up. For a minute I thought you
meant t'tea things! We say 'wash up' when it's t'plates, you
know. Dirty cutlery and that. But I – well, if you'll pardon the
expression, I *am* bursting. (*Pause.*) I don't like going, on trains.

  CLAIRE *smiles. She goes to the door leading upstairs.*

D

CLAIRE. It's upstairs. First landing, facing you.

FATHER *gets up and goes to the door.*

FATHER. Maybe I'd best go back. I shall only be in the way. (*Pause.*) And I am a bit confused, young lady.

CLAIRE. Mr Link – you'll stay. And see Bernard. And you'll be in nobody's way.

He smiles back at her, embarrassed. Then goes out. She comes downstage, sees the brown paper carrier. Picks it up. Puts her hand in. Comes out with a rolled pair of blue and white striped pyjamas. She stands looking at them, then replaces them in the carrier. Puts the carrier back exactly where he left it. She stands thinking, her face expressionless.

MR LINK reappears at the upstairs door. She jumps as he speaks.

FATHER. Why does it say Haggerty outside?

Pause.

CLAIRE. Outside?

FATHER. Beside t'door bell. Haggerty, it says. I thowt I'd come to t'wrong house.

Pause.

CLAIRE. It's a long story, Mr Link.

Pause.

FATHER. Oh. (*Pause.*) He'll have to get it changed, though, won't he? You can't have Haggerty when it's Link. Now can you?

CLAIRE. That's true –

Pause.

FATHER. Typical of our Bernard.

CLAIRE. Why?

FATHER. All you need is take that little card out. And put another one in saying Bernard Link. (*Pause.*) He's got no regard for the little things, hasn't Bernard. Me, I'd have had Link in that card slot afore I'd been in ten minutes. But that's me, isn't it? (*Pause.*) I've heard the name Haggerty. It's Irish.

CLAIRE. He isn't Irish.

FATHER. I don't like the Irish. They talk too much, and they'd rob a blind hen on a worm any day on t'week. (*Pause.*) He wants to get some cards *printed*, you know. He's not short o' brass. Printed. *LINK*. Nice big black letters. (*Pause*.) Don't want yon Haggerty's *bills* comin' here – now do we?

He vanishes upstairs again. CLAIRE *stands very still.*

CLAIRE. Get back quick, Haggerty. You're being *Linked*.

Curtain.

ACT TWO

Scene One

There have been small changes to the set since ACT ONE *– the decorating is nearly finished, and the shelves. Touches here and there demonstrating* CLAIRE'S *presence – perhaps a couple of pictures, flowers, rugs on the floor. Darkness, and sign lowered saying:* LONDON.

Fade up on BERNARD *sitting hunched on a chair with his raincoat on his knees. He is spotlit, the rest in darkness. He is scribbling in a small notebook balanced on his raincoat.*

The INTERPRETERS *from* ACT ONE *now double as* ACTORS – *three women and a man – dressed in the style of the Living Theatre. They circle* BERNARD'S *chair, whispering, the whispers becoming louder and louder.*

MAN. I am not allowed to travel without a passport.

1ST WOMAN. I cannot live without money.

2ND WOMAN. I am not allowed to take off my clothes.

3RD WOMAN. I am not allowed to smoke marijuana.

> BERNARD *scribbles away, as they circle, stop, address him and move on.*

3RD WOMAN. I cannot travel without a passport.

2ND WOMAN. I cannot live without money.

1ST WOMAN. I am not allowed to smoke marijuana.

MAN. I am not allowed to take my clothes off.

> *The last sequence is repeated in a loud shout, and* BERNARD *looks up furtively from his notes. The* THREE WOMEN *and the* MAN *break out in a rising cry of despair.*
>
> BERNARD *stuffs his notebook in his pocket, takes his raincoat*

*and comes downstage. The spot moves on him, leaving the chair
and the rest in darkness.*

BERNARD *stands a moment, looking shiftily from side to side
and clearing his throat. The* MAN *follows him and touches*
BERNARD'S *hand.*

MAN. Holy hands –

BERNARD. Er –

The MAN *touches his mouth.*

MAN. Holy mouth –

BERNARD. Well, I –

The MAN *touches his eyes.*

MAN. Holy eyes –

And by now thoroughly persecuted BERNARD *shifts his folded
raincoat in front of his genitals. But the* MAN *touches his head.*
Holy hair –

The MAN *exits.* BERNARD *is petrified, but a cynical jauntiness is
defensively pushing its way through. He stands very still for a
moment.*

BERNARD. Holy smoke!

Pause.

I'll bet they leave this country fully dressed. Passports firmly
gripped in paws. Cakes of hash in their tooth-paste tubes.
AND A LOT OF OUR MONEY!

Fade out and fade into

Scene Two

BERNARD'S FATHER *is sitting centre, in his characteristic position –
back straight, hands on knees. He stares expressionlessly in front of
himself. After a moment we hear a child howling upstairs. This fades
away. The hall door opens and* BERNARD *enters, fairly drunk.*

MR LINK *doesn't move a muscle.* BERNARD *stands swaying just
inside the room. Finally he circles unsteadily until he is front and
just left of his* FATHER.

BERNARD. I beg you not to lay formal charges until we reach the station. (*Pause.*) Even the long arm of the archetype must have its human side. What's more, I shall require the presence of my lawyer. (*Pause.*) I shall ring him before we leave this very room. And I warn you, he is no ordinary man. Any time of the night and day I can ring this lawyer and he will rush – through the night or day – to my rescue. The man is going mad from lack of sleep due to a surfeit of clients like me. And do you know why? Because he would rather be relied on than find the necessary and I might add wholly justifiable, violence within his gentle soul . . . he would rather be relied *on* than say, piss *off*.

   By this time BERNARD *is at the telephone with his hand on the receiver. His* FATHER, *still without moving, utters at last:*

FATHER. Drunk again!

   BERNARD, *struggling to co-ordinate, makes his way back across the room. He stands looking down at his* FATHER *for a long time. The old man now meets* BERNARD'S *eyes fair and square.*

BERNARD. I am holy. (*Pause.*) I am holy all over. (*Pause.*) I have been told so tonight. So don't have the *audacity* to start nagging a holy man.

   BERNARD *pulls forward a chair, sits down.*

FATHER. I thought you was supposed to be in Paris.

   Pause.

BERNARD. In Paris, I was, dad. And quick as a flash from the airport to earn my bread, being persecuted by a bunch of actors into a higher state of cynicism than ever before. (*Pause.*) No sign of Donald at the airport. New system now. Red sign for those with something to declare. Green sign for those whose avarice is properly confined within the area circumscribed by the law.

FATHER. Nay. In Paris, they said you was.

BERNARD. Would Donald be red – or green? Which colour would you say, in the circumstances, would offer most scope? After all, even when you go through the green they still have the right to pounce on you. Yes. Green for Donald. He's a pouncer.

(*Pause.*) No fun waiting on the red side for those who announce by the very direction of their tired feet that they have an excess of this-that-or-the-other in their suitcases.

Pause.

FATHER. I knew I shouldn't have stopped.

Pause.

BERNARD. Dad, it's four in the morning. I must admit that at least one other critic and I scuttled from the theatre to the nearest boozer. There to anaesthetise . . . even inhibit, as the saying goes . . . our shifty if complicated reactions to the evening's entertainment.

Pause.

FATHER. Pubs closes at eleven.

Pause.

BERNARD. Yes, indeed! But we made merry at my colleague's nearby house. Yea, until three and four in the morning. We drank all the way from holy to howly. What I mean is, I think one of us – possibly both – cried. We cried like men. America's messianic if cranky message . . . it got us, dad. It got us in the end. Poor weary tired sceptical old us. (*Pause.*) And speaking of America.

FATHER. It's just been yawlin' its head off.

BERNARD. America has?

FATHER. Well, I suppose he *is* American? In't he? T'baby? What with his mother being American, I had presumed that the father –

BERNARD. Hold on! Hang on! The question of the father will have to be gone into some other time. (*Pause.*) I just wanted to say, dad: how much it makes me feel at home to stagger in at four a.m. and find you sitting there with your hands on your knees. Waiting. Waiting waiting waiting. Time no object. We know, do we not, that sooner or later the door must open and the monster will come slithering across the room. Do we not? Know? Don't we?

Pause.

FATHER. Eh, Bernard! T'house is flooded.

  BERNARD *lifts up one foot and then the other.*

BERNARD. Maybe I *am* holy! Maybe I've been walking upon the
  water! But I don't see it.

  Pause.

FATHER. *My* house, lad.

  Pause.

BERNARD. Oh, damn and bugger it!

FATHER. There's no cause to go on like that.

BERNARD. Take no notice. It's a cry of rage against so much
  iniquity visited upon so much innocence.

  Pause.

FATHER. You what?

  Pause.

BERNARD. Dad. Has she taken care of you? Looked after you?

FATHER. The young lady?

BERNARD. Yes. Has she?

FATHER. By, I'll tell you. I've nowt but respect for that young
  woman. She's treated me like a king. (*Pause.*) We had summat
  called pumpkin pie for afters last night. I thought it were a bit
  queer at first, but I got to like it after a couple of spoonfuls.

BERNARD. Pumpkin pie, dad, is to America what Yorkshire
  pudding is to the West Riding. (*Pause.*) How many times do
  you have to get flooded before you shift out of that house?

  Pause.

FATHER. I'm stopping in yon house. (*Pause.*) Your mother
  wouldn't like it. Me going. Not after all those years.

  Pause.

BERNARD. Funny.

FATHER. What is?

BERNARD. Well, I mean, with me mother being dead. I mean, can
  a dead person continue to like or dislike . . . I mean –

FATHER. I *know* what you mean. I've heard it before. (*Pause.*)
  And *you* know what *I* mean.

  Pause.

BERNARD. True.

    Pause.

FATHER. Well, you've got a reight going on here. Haven't you?
(*Pause: leans forward.*) I don't know what you doing wi' a
'omosexual prancing round t'place. (*Pause.*) Mind. Chris seems
a straightforward young feller. (*Pause: looking round.*) I liked it
better in Hampstead. More air in Hampstead. Higher. More
green. (*Pause.*) But it's a lovely baby. (*Pause.*) Bit of a yawler.
(*Pause.*) *You* were a bit on a yawler. (*Pause.*) It's not a bad
thing in a baby. (*Pause.*) Gets t'oxygen into their lungs, you
know.

BERNARD. Does it?

    Pause.

FATHER. There's more *oxygen*, up Hampstead way.

    Pause.

BERNARD. You ever come across the name Raskolnikov before?

FATHER. Can't say I have, lad.

BERNARD. Well, that's its name. The baby's name.

    Pause.

FATHER. That certainly clears up one mystery.

BERNARD. Does it?

FATHER. Well, I take it that Rass is short for Rask-whatever-you-
said. (*Pause.*) And I had wondered what sort of a name Rass
might be. Her referring to the child by that name. And I
didn't wish to intrude by inquiring any further. (*Pause.*)
She's a fine young woman. She is entitled to name her bairn
according to her wishes. (*Pause.*) Or the father's.

    *There is a really piercing, long howl upstairs. They both listen.
    After a few moments the cries fade, then* CLAIRE *enters in a
    housecoat.* BERNARD'S FATHER *smiles at her.*

Making a reight din tonight, in't he?

    CLAIRE *crosses to* BERNARD, *as she answers,* MR LINK.

CLAIRE (*to* FATHER). He's eaten some of the fur off his monkey.

FATHER. The little devil!

CLAIRE. Welcome home stranger!

They confront each other in silence for a few seconds. MR LINK *sits, looking ahead.*

FATHER. Aye. He's back. And none too sober.

BERNARD *crosses slowly to* CLAIRE. *Kisses her gently on the cheek. He turns, spreading his arms wide.*

BERNARD. Here we are at last. Our heterogeneous little family. All under one roof. At last. (*Pause.*) Leaping from the taxi outside, I ached for solitude. But that was selfish. Welcome home, *all* you strangers!

FATHER. It's not one over the eight wi' him! It's eight over the bloody twenty.

CLAIRE. Mr Link! I said not to wait up –

FATHER. What I often think to mesen is: if he'd just think on his dad when he 'as that one too many – he wouldn't. If he'd just think on t'effect on his father.

BERNARD. If I thought of you when drinking, dad, I'd be dead from cirrhosis of the liver.

CLAIRE *looks stonily at* BERNARD *and goes into the kitchen.*

CLAIRE (*exiting*). Rass's spewing it at both ends.

Pause.

FATHER. I'll get meself upstairs, then. 'Appen you'll be in a more fit state in the morning. (*He stands up, hesitating.*)

BERNARD. I'll drive you up to Yorkshire, dad. We'll get the house fixed. Only I wish you'd *move*!

FATHER. Get it fixed? Does't think I've lost t'use on me own two hands, then?

Pause.

BERNARD. Dad – I'm pleased to see you.

FATHER. Aye. I've no doubt. Wi' a skinful o' whisky inside thee!

BERNARD. Ah, dad! War, famine, pestilence, murder, injustice, capitalism in crisis, Stalinism tightening the screws harder and harder. And on top of it all, being a bloody theatre critic! If you'd gone through what I went through tonight –

FATHER. I fired engines nigh on fifteen year. I drove expresses thirty-five year, wi'all them people's lives behind me. And I never took a drop. As for t'theatre I've none gotten further than seeing Mother Duck at Leeds pantomine. Don't look at me for no sympathy!

BERNARD. I agree. It would be futile.

Pause.

FATHER. I'll say goodnight, then.

Pause.

BERNARD. Goodnight, dad. Throttle up those expresses in the old roaring dreams.

FATHER. When I dream. Which is not very often. I dream on thy mother.

He goes out, upstairs. CLAIRE *enters with nappies over her arm.* BERNARD *sits staring belligerently after his father.*

BERNARD. Imagine living with her forty years then dreaming with her for the rest of your life! Nobody could say my mother was one to let a little thing like dying stand in the way. In the way of. Of her.

CLAIRE *sits down tiredly with the nappies.*

CLAIRE. He sure brings out another side of you, Bernard!

BERNARD. I've got my facets. I have got my facets. (*Pause.*) Lurking.

Pause.

CLAIRE. Rass's quiet. (*Pause.*) Jesus, I'm screwed! (*Pause.*) So how was Paris? I made some coffee in the kitchen. You want some?

BERNARD. I wouldn't mind. Yes, please.

She goes into the kitchen and comes back with coffee. BERNARD *sits sipping his. She stretches out exhausted in her chair, the coffee on her lap.*

Floods! He's got floods! I've got floods. My sanity needs a bleeding Noah's Ark. (*Long pause.*) I found a few things out about Haggerty in Paris. Quite by accident, really.

CLAIRE (*sitting up straight, alert*). Well, come *on*, then –

Pause.

BERNARD. First of all, there were these telegrams from Paris. From him.

CLAIRE. Yeah. Chris told me after you left. Sounded authentic Haggerty all right.

Pause.

BERNARD. Well, in Paris, I met a lecturer who'd known him a week or two. It seems Haggerty . . . did he have any money by the way?

CLAIRE. A few thousand dollars when he left New York for London. (*Pause.*) My money, needless to say. (*Pause.*) What the hell! *My* money was my father's money. And any way of using it to besmirch his dear old memory suits me. I mean, any way subversively disposing of that graceful Republican hypocrite's cash! Both Haggerty and I are well qualified.

Pause.

BERNARD. It seems . . . Haggerty left Paris. And he left a man acting for him as a kind of agent. With some money, and a peculiar list of instructions – which included the telegrams.

Pause.

CLAIRE. What are we to live in fear and trembling of besides the telegrams?

BERNARD. That he wouldn't say. (*Pause.*) Scrutinizing me in relation to the whole arrangement, he looked . . . smug. (*Pause.*) Vulpine. (*Pause.*) He kept on wiping his mouth with a handkerchief and looking at me pityingly. Some kind of lawyer. Nothing illegal was involved, he archly informed me.

CLAIRE. And the fiendish Haggerty disappeared to *where*?

BERNARD. I do not know, Monsieur. It is not of my business. The man said. (*Pause.*) Who is now sleeping where, by the way?

CLAIRE. Unless you have a kind of yen to sleep with your father – (*Points at a divan.*) I made up a bed there.

Pause.

BERNARD. I don't know why I don't just move out. For a while. For ever. (*Pause.*) What if Haggerty's fixer-man in Paris sent us a bomb?

CLAIRE. Nothing illegal, remember?

BERNARD. Oh, yes. Still. You and I haven't exactly worked out a modus vivendi yet. Have we? (*Pause.*) You had me in a state of shock for days! (*Pause.*) Of course, I realize coming here and finding the flat –

CLAIRE. Oh, for Christ's sake, Bernard! I'm going to bed. (*She goes to the door, with the nappies.*)

Want to bed down in Rass's room? Got a supply of ear plugs and nose filters?

Pause.

BERNARD. *Good night!*

CLAIRE *exits.* BERNARD *finishes his coffee. Wanders over to the divan. Kicks it. Turns back the covers. He sits down and takes his shoes off. Then his trousers. Half fills a glass of whisky. Takes the desk lamp to the divan side. Climbs into bed. Raises his glass.*

Thus we launch our frail coracle into the night! (*He drains the whisky. Puts out the light.*)

Scene Three

Sign lowered saying: CHICAGO.

A spot picks out CLAIRE, *the rest of the stage in darkness. Her hair is tied back. She looks much younger. Her dress is in a fashion of fourteen years ago. She calls out:*

CLAIRE. James –

She pulls up a chair and sits down. She is fiddling with her hair. She looks up.

James Mawnan Haggerty, *I'm* going to call you 'Haggerty' from now on. (*Pause.*) Look. OK. You take the newspaper into the john. OK. D'you have to bring it out? (*Pause.*) I mean, we just ran away together. We arrive. I mean, we haven't un-packed and you vanish into the john. With a *newspaper*! (*Pause.*) Haggerty, I will not have you sit in front of me reading. I wouldn't

care if it was . . . if it was *anything* else. But *reading*! (*Pause.*)
It's not a passionate thing to do. Budapest? (*Long pause.*)
Geography I am weak on. (*Pause.*) They're doing what? (*Pause.*)
Haggerty I am *seventeen* and I do not even grasp America.
James Mawnan! Huh! Was it your mammy or your daddy
stuck you with those two pins. (*Pause.*) When you raise your
eyeballs over the top of the paper you know what you look like?
Two large plonks of bird shit rolling on a wire! (*Pause.*) I dig
you are conveying antagonism. (*Pause.*) Already. (*Looks at her
watch.*) We have been alone together in our new life for sixteen
and one quarter minutes. (*Pause.*) I *know* my vernacular is not
that of rich daddy's background and status. (*Pause.*) I mix my
vernaculars because I am an adolescent in a condition of revolt.
(*Pause.*) Is what is going on in Budapest passionate, I want to
know? I mean screw the political angle, I just want to have a
kind of guideline whose side I'm on. (*Pause.*) *Both* sides are
communist? (*Pause.*) I am reduced to awed silence. (*Pause.*)
Who'd elope to *Chicago*? (*Pause.*) Yeah! But *I* wasn't born here!
And what did it do for you? (*Pause.*) I know I've a lot to learn.
(*Pause.*) And you'll have to do the educating, won't you? I
mean, being here with you isn't exactly a passport to Vassar –
is it? (*Pause.*) Haggerty, I *told* you. I *invented* the way I talk.
It is calculated to negate my background and suggest whorish
undertones. (*Pause.*) If I take all my clothes off will you put that
goddam paper down? (*Pause.*) Russians? Tanks? Christ, I've
hardly gotten over the English knocking hell out of the Arabs!
(*Pause.*) How is one to *orientate*, man? (*Pause.*) Haggerty, I
am going to remove my clothes and lie on that crummy stinking
bed and open my legs. Should you continue to ingest foreign
news so stubbornly. I shall then hit you with a chair. (*Pause.*)
Haggerty, I love you. I want you. (*Pause.*) I think I am going to
cry.

   Fade out and fade in to

Scene Four

The following day. Afternoon. CHRIS *is wiring a new socket for the hi-fi equipment.* ROGER, *precarious on a three-step aluminium ladder is ronsealing the new shelves.* MR LINK *sits centre, his nose tipped with a pair of glasses, a newspaper on his knees. But he is staring into space.* CLAIRE *enters, switches on the vacuum already plugged in and starts cleaning. There is a definite atmosphere in the room. She comes to* MR LINK – *he lifts his feet. She vacuums under his chair and he puts his feet down again. She stops working and goes into the kitchen: comes out with a beer.*

CLAIRE. Want a beer Mr Link?

FATHER. No thanks, love.

CLAIRE (*negligently*). Beer, anybody?

CHRIS. I will when I've got this wired up. It's tricky.

CLAIRE (*looking up at* ROGER). Tinkerbell?

ROGER (*brushing and not looking at her*). If you mean *me* dear, I'm not a beer person at all. (*Turns, and looks down at her.*) I don't like beer, twinklecrutch dearie –

CLAIRE. God, that stuff you're putting on stinks!

ROGER (*busy*). If Bernard wants his shelves ronsealed – ronsealed they shall be. And you may have noticed, though I doubt it, I seem to come in for the stinky jobs. Nobody has to tell *me* I'm not a genius with the carpentry. These hands were meant for finer things.

CLAIRE. Yeah! Like –

ROGER (*quickly and firmly, looking at* MR LINK). Pas devant les pères, s'il vous plaît, dear!

    Pause.

FATHER. Always beats me why they don't never seem to get on –

CLAIRE. Who doesn't?

FATHER. Women and 'omosexuals. They'd 'ave summat in common, you'd think. Always biting each other's noses, you two are,

(*Pause.*) I've been thinking it over. I suppose we 'ave them up north. Have 'omos, I mean. But you never seem to come across it. I've never come across it, not up north. (*Pause.*) And another thing. Considering Bernard's comfortably off and you're well set up yourself, young lady, why not 'ave somebody in to clean? (*Pause.*) I have one, you know. Home help. Every Wednesday. (*Pause.*) Pinched one on his mother's hats. I nearly went up t-Town Hall about it, but I can't prove nothing. Wait till I see her wearing that hat in t'town one on these Fridays when I'm doing me shopping. (*Pause.*) I'll rip it off her bloody head. (*Pause.*) She's one on them as cleans *round* things. Never thinks on going underneath. You'd think there wasn't no such thing as underneath. (*Pause.*) But that's where all t'fluff is.

CLAIRE. You kept Mrs Link's hats ever since she died?

FATHER. I kept *that* 'at.

ROGER. Was it a gorgeous one?

    Pause.

FATHER. It was round. And all made on fur. (*Pause.*) Our Bernard brought it back from Moscow for her. His first trip that were. (*Pause.*) Best thing 'at come out on Moscow, if you ask me. (*Pause.*) She was a bonny woman. (*Pause.*) A bit over-weight. (*Pause.*) Sixteen stone. (*Pause.*) But she looked a treat in that Russian 'at. (*Pause.*) You be surprised how many women on my generation was overweight. Now why would that be? (*Pause.*) Ate nowt but bread and bugger all else for many a long year, for one thing. (*Pause.*) Joint on a Sunday. Then rissoles from t'joint on a Monday. (*Pause.*) Course, railwaymen was better off than a lot. (*Pause.*) The aristocracy of the working class, my father used to say. And he was a miner. (*Pause.*) It was the railwaymen broke the general strike, you know. (*Pause.*) Union solidarity's one thing. To watch your bairns go 'ungry and listen to the wife nagging – that's another. (*Pause.*) Three things buggered the strikes: hungry bairns, shame, and nagging bloody women! (*Pause.*) There wasn't a woman with a 'at from Moscow in our village! No. And I shouldn't think in Doncaster either. (*Pause.*)

That's always our Bernard's way: hand out a few quid, buy summat useless from Roumania or somewhere. And goodbye to owt else! (*Pause.*) A lot had their wombs taken away, an' all. Summat 'appens to a woman that's had her womb taken away.

ROGER. Hormones.

FATHER. Eh?

ROGER. Sort of chemicals in the body, Mr Link. We're all at the mercy of these nasty little molecules. (*Pause : tartly.*) Including 'omos!

> CLAIRE *deliberately starts vacuuming again.* MR LINK *lifts up his paper.*

FATHER (*shouting*). I brought him t'Gazette, an' all –

> CLAIRE *stops vacuuming.* CHRIS *goes into the kitchen for a beer, returning.*

CLAIRE. I beg your pardon?

FATHER. Last week's local Gazette. I brought it down for him. Might as well bring a bicycle for a bloke wi' no legs! Listen to this: Gordon Carghill was remanded on bail after police investigations at Stanhill Mental Hospital. (*Pause.*) I should bloody think he was, an' all. (*Pause.*) Him and our Bernard was at Junior School together and their Gordon – well, he was a bad-un from t'start. (*Pause.*) Wonder what he was getting up to at mental hospital? Charge nurse, an' all. (*Pause.*) He used to pinch rhubarb out on my allotment. You can always tell the way they going to go. (*Pause.*) Rhubarb an' custard. (*Pause.*) I don't suppose that would be a national dish in your country, young lady? I mean, like t'pumpkin pie?

CLAIRE. I guess not, Mr Link.

> *There is a long silence.* MR LINK *studies the paper.*

FATHER. Floods expected to subside within a few days! We've heard that one before! (*Pause.*) Floods goes but rats doesn't. (*Pause.*) I used to 'ave a little terrier could snap a rat's neck like a twig! (*Pause.*) Lots of whippets round our way. (*Pause.*) I never liked whippets. (*Pause.*) 'Course, it *is* a miner's dog.

(*Pause.*) Them and greyhounds. (*Pause.*) I can't bide greyhounds either. Ribs sticking through. Wrap theirsens round your
legs like a mucky wet rag. (*Pause.*) A terrier's a reliable dog,
though. Hardy. (*Pause.*) It's the *gambling* gets me, wi' greyhounds and whippets! (*Pause.*) I wouldn't never gamble. Summat for nowt. That's what they all want. (*Pause.*) Now a pigeon's
a different thing. They gamble as well on pigeons. But it's the
bird itself. (*Pause.*) A lovely bird.

> CLAIRE, ROGER *and* CHRIS *are transfixed by the old man's
> monologue. Helpless, not wanting to stop him or hurt him – he
> simply represents a world stubbornly impervious to their experi-
> ence.*

> BERNARD *enters, holding a small yellow telegram envelope.
> He stands looking at the little group.* MR LINK *is quite unaware
> of his effect on the people around him.*

Did you get my bacca?

BERNARD (*looking at the others*). Yes, I got your bacca. (*Pause.*)
You all seem a bit subdued –

> CHRIS *goes back to working on the socket, his beer beside him.*
> ROGER *brushes away at his shelves.*

ROGER. Mr Link's been telling us all about whippets and pigeons.
(*Pause.*) And hats. (*Pause.*) Ever so absorbing.

> MR LINK *opens his tobacco tin.*

FATHER. I'm down to a couple o' dog ends. (*Pause.*) What I do,
I put me dog ends in me tin. Then when I've got enough I make
them up into cigs.

BERNARD (*coming forward*). Here's your tobacco, dad. (*Pause.*)
What hats?

FATHER. That one on your mother's t'home help pinched.

> *Pause.*

BERNARD. You don't know whether she pinched it or not. And
I'm sure she didn't.

FATHER. Ah, they'd fiddle owt off you when you're on your own.
Think you're daft in t'head or summat. Can't see a hat when
it's missing! (*Pause.*) I liked home help I had afore her. Now *she*

went underneath! (*Pause.*) Dropped dead in Woolworth's it'll be eight month now. (*Pause.*) I don't like to see Claire vacuuming round, neither. What happened to that woman you had in Hampstead?

BERNARD. They . . . they, you know, come and go. In London.

CLAIRE *has been watching and listening to all this impassively.*
MR LINK *peers at her over his glasses.*

FATHER. Caught *that* one smoking when she were frying his bacon and eggs one morning. (*Pause.*) Up Hampstead. (*Pause.*) That's southerners for you! Smoking when they cooking. (*Pause.*) Cig dangling out on her mouth whenever you looked at her. (*Pause.*) It's disgusting in a woman. (*Pause.*) At all times.
Pause.

CLAIRE. I smoke, Mr Link –

FATHER (*to* BERNARD). You'll not have bothered to look at Gazette?

BERNARD. No, dad.

FATHER. Police is investigating Gordon Carghill for summat.

BERNARD. Never heard of him.

FATHER. No. You wouldn't have. He just sat next to you at same desk at Junior School.
Pause.

BERNARD. Thirty-five years ago.

FATHER. What difference does that make? You. You remember nowt and nobody. And care neither! Well, it's all here in t'-Gazette.

CLAIRE. Bernard –

BERNARD. What?

CLAIRE. I think you're holding a telegram.
He looks down at it as if he's never seen it.

BERNARD. Oh, yes. (*Pause.*) Yes. (*He opens the telegram and stands looking at it.*)

CLAIRE. Haggerty?
BERNARD *makes for the door to the stairs.*
Read it, Bernard –

BERNARD *stops, turns, hesitating.*

FATHER. Waste o' good money, telegrams. Catch me sending
one. It all goes to t'Government. (*Pause.*) Then there's the little
matter of it being our Bernard's own business no doubt. If
you'll pardon me. I don't like to interfere.

BERNARD. You once opened a letter of mine and read it!

Pause.

FATHER(*flatly*). You was under twenty-one. (*Pause.*) Your mother
and me was deeply shocked. (To CLAIRE.) He 'ad a young girl
pregnant. That one! That one over there! I've never seen such a
letter in all my life. (*Pause.*) Straight into t'fire wi' *that* letter!

Pause.

CLAIRE. And the girl?

FATHER. She'd borrowed some money and had a abortion. (*To*
BERNARD.) Dirty young devil! (*Pause.*) It grieves me to think
about it now, even after all this time. (*Pause.*) We didn't know
the *half* on what *he* did when he left home.

He lifts his paper, emanating his twenty-four-year-old grief.
BERNARD *holds up the telegram, reading it out to* CLAIRE.

BERNARD. Yes, it's Haggerty. It says: PREDICT THE BITCH
WILL NOW BE DUG IN STOP (*Pause.*) HOPE YOU CARRIED
OUT STRATEGY OF SUBMISSION BECAUSE NOW IS TIME
EJECT THE NEUROTIC BUNDLE FROM YOUR FOXHOLE
STOP (*Pause.*) REMEMBER JUNG VERSUS J. JOYCE RE
JOYCE'S DAUGHTER STOP (*Pause.*) YOU ARE A DEEP SEA
DIVER MISTER JOYCE BUT YOUR DAUGHTER IS DROWN-
ING STOP (*Pause.*) WISH HAD KNOWN YOU BERNARD
STOP (*Pause.*) READ SOME OF YOUR ACID THEATRE RE-
VIEWS STOP (*Pause.*) RESEARCHED YOU FULLY STOP FACT
IS I SYMPATHISE WITH YOU RE CLAIRE STOP (*Pause.*)
REGARD HER NOW WITH CLINICAL DETACHMENT AS A
MERE SPECIMEN STOP (*Pause.*) YOU WILL NOT UNDER-
STAND AMERICA BUT NEITHER DOES SHE STOP (*Pause.*)
PULL RASS'S NOSE FOR ME STOP (*Pause.*) HERE ON DE-
ESCALATION OF TELEGRAMS STOP (*Pause.*) HAGGERTY.

Long pause.

ROGER. Cheek!

FATHER. Brazen, I'd call it. Not that I can make head nor tail on it. But it gives off a sort on a brazen impression, like.

Pause.

CLAIRE. Mr Link. The substance of the impression is true. But about me not Haggerty. I mean so far as Bernard is concerned. (*Pause.*) All your son did was lease a flat. And who brought Rely-On into Bernard's life? Well, that *was* Haggerty. Then me, Rass, and –

FATHER. *I* come on me own accord. I always do.

Pause.

BERNARD. It says in this morning's paper the floods went down yesterday.

Pause.

FATHER. I can take a hint.

BERNARD. I didn't mean that.

Pause.

FATHER (*staring in front*). He's always been on his own before. (*Pause.*) Bit of a hermit, like. (*Pause.*) Never managed to make a right home. Keep a good woman. (*Pause.*) *I* think there's summat up wi' our Bernard. (*Laughs to himself.*) Owt to put him in Stanhill Asylum and let Gordon Carghill knock a bit o' sense into him! (*He turns to* BERNARD.) Tha lets people tread all over thee! (*Turns to* CLAIRE.) And I'm not speaking on you, love.

CHRIS *stands up from his work, finishing his beer.*

CHRIS. Haggerty recommended Bernard to Rely-On because of me. (*Pause.*) I'm not boasting. (*Pause.*) He knew I was leaving the other firm, and he knew I'd see Bernard right with the work. (*Pause.*) I told him I was a drifter. (*Pause.*) I like to move about a bit. Always do a good job. Painting, wiring, plumbing. You name it, I can do it.

BERNARD. Why should Haggerty *care*? About whether I get good workmanship or not?

Pause.

CHRIS. He liked good workmanship. (*Pause.*) I expect he'd knocked about a bit in America before he met Claire. (*Turns to look up at* ROGER *on the ladder.*) 'Course I've no idea if he knew the sort o' talent they *get* at Rely-On.

Pause.

FATHER. I think I'll take mesen out a bit. (*Pause.*) Have a bit of a walk. (*Pause.*) Not that it isn't muggy down here compared with Hampstead.

They all watch him get up in silence, acknowledging the old man's rough tact. He puts his jacket on and takes his hat.

(*To* BERNARD, *nodding at* CLAIRE.) I told her. You want to shift yon one's name off t'door.

CLAIRE. Mr Link, I only came here because I thought Haggerty'd *be* here. We *lived* here before I went back to New York and had Rass –

FATHER. By – you fell over yoursen to get back after t'little lad were born, didn't you? (*Pause.*) But it's none on my affair, young lady.

He goes out. BERNARD *still stands weakly by the door leading upstairs.*

We hear the baby start howling. BERNARD *goes out and upstairs followed by* CLAIRE. ROGER *comes down off the ladder to* CHRIS.

ROGER (*menacingly, for him*). I think it's time we cleared the air, dear. You and me.

Pause.

CHRIS. Take a bit o' clearing, the air round here!

ROGER. *You* know what I mean!

Pause.

CHRIS. Do I carry you on my back on these jobs or not?

Pause.

ROGER (*sulkily*). Well. What if you do?

Pause.

CHRIS. Bernard's not interested, you know.

ROGER *puts the ronseal tin down. Lays the brush across the top.*

ROGER. I know. (*He starts crying.*) Jimmy threw me out last night. (*Pause.*) Said he was going away for two days. (*Pause.*) Well, it's been quite unpleasant between us for a week or two. Anyway, he came back a day early. And who's upstairs with a *divine* spade?

CHRIS (*drily*). Little old Rodge.

ROGER. Yes. Little old Rodge. D'you know Jimmy actually *kicked* me? Down the stairs? And threw all my things down as well. (*Pause.*) I mean I thought if *she* went. I thought Bernard might –

Pause.

CHRIS. She'll go before long. She's not here to squeeze Bernard. (*Pause.*) And *you're* not going to squeeze him either –

Pause.

ROGER. God! One might think you were a bit Bernard inclined yourself the way you talk!

Pause.

CHRIS (*quietly*). Put the ronseal brush in the tin of white spirits in the kitchen. And we'll knock off for today. (*Pause.*) It's Bernard's old man that gets me. (*Pause.*) I mean, sitting there like he does. And coming out with all that ramble. (*Pause.*) He upsets me, you know?

ROGER *takes the brush into the kitchen.* CHRIS *tidies the corner where he's been working and puts some tools into an open leather bag.* ROGER *comes in, looking a little brighter.*

There's a room going where I live. Paddington way. (*Pause.*) Four quid a week. (*He grins.*) House full of spades –

ROGER. Oh, Chrissy! (*Pause.*) One can't *think* how it's all going to end up here.

CHRIS. I don't know. (*Pause.*) You never know. (*Pause.*) For my money, Haggerty'll walk in through that door one of these days.

ROGER. And *then* what?

CHRIS. Work it out. Look at her. Listen to her. (*Pause.*) That bird'll walk out the door with Haggerty and the kid.

Pause.

ROGER. Poor old Bernard!

    ROGER *pulls on a sweater.* CHRIS *gets his old reefer jacket. They exit.*

    Fade out and fade in to

Scene Five

Darkness. A sign is lowered saying : NEW YORK.

    An empty chair is spotlit. CLAIRE *enters, wearing a light raincoat. She looks round. Takes off the raincoat : underneath, a white summer dress, bloodstained.* CLAIRE *has blood on one side of her face. She curls up in the chair, hugging herself in her arms. After a moment, she sits up and turns towards the audience.*

CLAIRE. Don't say it, Haggerty! Yes. OK. The demonstrations are shit. The marches are shit. (*Pause.*) The sit-ins were a start. Then *you* get all high and mighty. And we end up you studying guerrilla warfare in the pad and me getting beaten to hell in the streets. (*Pause.*) Well, *look* at me, will you? (*Pause.*) I'm lucky I wasn't busted! (*Pause.*) No, I *don't* want you to clean me up, and kiss me, and screw me into submission. I want to just sit here, man, and be *bloody*. (*Long pause.*) God, it's been rough with you! And I go on and on and on and on! (*Pause.*) Well, I did get tougher, didn't I? And less stupid? And read a million books? (*Pause.*) Sure. Leaves Vassar standing. I sometimes dream that's *where* I'm standing: in Vassar. And *loving* it. (*Pause.*) And I wish you were in Cuba, or on goddam Mars or somewhere. (*Pause.*) Haggerty, you don't stir a *toe* any more. You preparing for civil war out of a book? (*Pause.*) Listen, after all you said it first: America'll rook you or cook you. And in the meantime we sit on our fannys? (*Pause.*) Honey, no! Don't touch me. I'll get in the bath and stick me up with a band-aid. (*Pause.*) Jesus, it's hot! And I bounced out of that tangle like a kangaroo. (*Pause.*) I am *not* crying – it's tear gas. (*Pause.*) Hell,

I'm crying as well. Tear gas tears and me tears. Because I feel like I'm going to crack. Split. Wham! Right down the middle. (*Pause.*) Yeah. I know. Half the kids at school with me are on the shrink's couch by now. So who needs a shrink when there's life with you? (*Pause.*) *Life!* (*Pause.*) Next summer Oakland. Next summer somewhere else. (*Pause.*) Any sonofabitch calls me a white liberal after all this, I'm gonna carve his goddam eyes out. (*Pause.*) Just give me a couple months and I'll be a black fascist. (*Pause.*) Whilst you brood!

> CLAIRE *gets up from the chair and comes downstage, followed by the spot.*

Can we just go to my place at Amagansett? For a week-end, or something? And just swim. And lie in the sun? (*Pause.*) Do you need me at all? (*Pause.*) Have I, in trying to become something for you and then seeing it for myself . . . have I become a kind of *joke*? (*Pause.*) Not that you ever laugh. (*Pause.*) You used to. (*Pause.*) I mean, are we still human? As well as humanity? (*Pause.*) Do you know that now I can see with your eyes? Hear with your ears? Spit with your tongue? (*Pause.*) That I am inside your *head*, Haggerty? (*Pause.*) Does it *corrupt* you or something? (*Pause.*) But I am as separate, and hard, and knowledgeable as you could wish. (*Pause.*) Will you hold me? (*Pause.*) Will you lick this blood off my face? (*Pause.*) Will you permit me one hour's *peace*?

> *Fade out and fade in to*

Scene Six

BERNARD'S *room.* MR LINK *sits in his chair, a paper on his knees, his head thrown back. He is asleep and snoring gently. To one side of him:* BERNARD, *smoking and staring into space. To the other side:* CLAIRE, *with a drink, also staring ahead, over* BERNARD'S *shoulder. It is after lunch.*

CLAIRE. Thank God he sleeps plenty.

BERNARD. Yeh.

Pause.

CLAIRE. You know the steak?

BERNARD. What steak?

CLAIRE. We had *steak* for lunch. You remember? That kind of brown triangle with black grill marks on it you ate? That was steak.

Pause.

BERNARD. Oh. (*Pause.*) Yes.

CLAIRE. He bought it.

BERNARD. I know.

CLAIRE. How d'you know?

BERNARD. It's like a sort of perverse gift. I can always recognise steak me dad bought.

CLAIRE. He spends an awful lot of time talking about meat.

BERNARD. Yes. He's a butcher manqué. Shove him out in the fields, he doesn't see animals. He sees cuts.

Pause.

CLAIRE. Does he make a habit of visiting you when he's *not* flooded?

Pause.

BERNARD. It started about two years ago. He just turns up. And sits. And watches. (*Pause.*) If I'm drunk, I mock him. (*Pause.*) If I'm sober I spend half the time lying and the other half apologising for having turned out badly. (*Pause.*) He's only got to walk in through the door and I can make regression look like progress compared with my bloody performance.

MR LINK *wakes up with a twitch and sits straight.*

FATHER. Insects.

BERNARD. Who? Us?

Pause.

FATHER. I were thinking.

BERNARD. You were sleeping.

FATHER. Do you think I don't know t'difference in mesen?

BERNARD. I could imagine you having genuine difficulties in making a distinction.

FATHER. Does t'ever understand what he's on about, Claire?

CLAIRE (*laughing*). Oh, I don't know. I guess so.

>   *Pause.*

FATHER. I was *thinking*. On a summer evening many a long year ago. (*Pause.*) Were only a fireman then. (*Pause.*) We was taking this goods train up a long gradient, right out in t'country. (*Pause.*) I had t'firebox door open and we went through a great cloud on them little gnats. They got caught up in the hot air. And it consumed them. (*Pause.*) Thousands on tiny little bodies going up in the air, like sparks, you know. (*Pause.*) By, they do bring me out in bumps if they get me when I'm fishing.

>   *Pause.*

BERNARD. Nice piece of steak, dad.

FATHER. I thought you'd appreciate it.

BERNARD. Plenty of nice fat and gristle.

FATHER. Meat's nowt wi'out a bit of fat.

BERNARD. That's right. And what's more, I still can't spit it out.

FATHER. You what?

BERNARD. When I was a kid, you used to make me sit and chew it till I was crying and spewing at the same time. Get it down thee! It's what puts t'muscles on. (*Holds up his arm.*) Look at that arm nearly forty years later. If you can find a muscle I'll give you ten quid.

FATHER. That's because tha spends thy time on thy backside. Tchah! Theatre critic! (*Pause.*) Now if folks like George Formby an' Gracie Fields was still going! That *was* entertainment. (*Pause.*) I suppose they was well known in America as well. (*To* CLAIRE.) But you'd be too young, love. It's all jitterbugging now over there. In't it?

BERNARD. Dad –

FATHER. What, lad?

BERNARD. Have you noticed –

>   *Pause.*

FATHER. What?

BERNARD. You spend quite a bit of time on *your* backside. In that chair, for example.

Pause.

FATHER (*shouts*). I'm retired!

BERNARD. You don't sit because you're retired. Or old. Or ill or weak. (*Stands up, speaking wickedly.*) You sit because nothing moves or stirs within! Nothing triggers off the old vaso-motor system, does it? A leg here, an arm there. A meaningful rotation of the eyeballs. Eh? Not a bloody quiver!

MR LINK *has probably heard a lot of this kind of thing before – but not in front of a third person. He folds his paper. Slowly gets up. Lumbers to the stairs door. Looks at* BERNARD, *then* CLAIRE.

FATHER. What it is, young lady. Our Bernard doesn't like me, you see. He doesn't even *like* me –

He goes out. BERNARD *flops back into his chair.* CLAIRE, *angry, goes to the window.*

CLAIRE. You wouldn't even talk to that little fag actor like that.

Pause.

BERNARD. Everything in its proper place. Including spleen. (*Pause.*) And be careful. Don't go for me. (*Pause.*) You know a thousand times less about him and me than I do about Harlem!

CLAIRE (*acidly*). Does it all go back to the dark satanic mills, honey?

BERNARD. Oh, piss off –

Pause.

CLAIRE. I *am* going, soon.

Pause.

BERNARD. *Right.*

Pause.

CLAIRE. Bernard –

Pause.

BERNARD (*quietly*). Do you think he doesn't nearly make me bloody *cry*?

Pause.

CLAIRE. Bernard, once I moved in here – I never did a damn thing about tracing Haggerty. (*Points.*) I arrived at that door fuming. And you caught it. And I'm sorry. (*She sits in the chair vacated by* MR LINK.)

BERNARD. Did you really think he was still in London?

Pause.

CLAIRE. I thought he might be.

BERNARD. And if he had been?

Pause.

CLAIRE. I guess I'd have tried to force the usual things on him. (*Pause.*) Fourteen years of me stuck in my groove. (*Grimacing.*) Very *un*groovy! (*Pause.*) Me yelling, whining, loving. And that man so still. So quiet. So . . . secret. (*Pause.*) But he could slice my head off with one word. And me? I'd stand up spouting blood and show him my head on a platter and bawl: look what you *done* to me, Haggerty –

BERNARD (*not ungently*). It's what they call being a slow developer. I haven't developed at all. Still the same chubby little lad Mam packed off to school. (*Pause.*) After threatening to put me in the orphanage for being bad. (*Pause.*) If I'd been bright, I'd have realized she might have a problem with the orphanage. I mean, proving she and me dad were dead. (*Pause.*) Well, at least you stuck out fourteen years with Haggerty. I split my stint into two sevens with two women. (*Pause.*) Didn't seem to dilute my sheer inadequacy for either of them. (*He gets up. Goes to her.*) *I* thought I took your melodramatic descent with a . . . with a certain lugubriousness. Considering.

CLAIRE. Yeah. That was very deceitful of you.

BERNARD. Why?

Pause.

CLAIRE. It kind of deflated me. In the end. (*Pause.*) You don't resist, Bernard. You absorb. That's highly dangerous. (*Pause.*) Your old man isn't so dumb! *He* said you'd – God give me the dialect – he said you'd 'niver kept a good wooooman'.

Pause.

BERNARD. Aside from the irrelevance of dadda's ethics, it's true. (*Pause.*) He's a trifle behind on quaint contemporary issues like your autonomy, your independence, your self-liberation and your women in society and all that.

CLAIRE. *All that!* Man, I've kicked it!

Pause.

BERNARD. I don't think I'm very far in front of him, either.

Pause.

CLAIRE. *God,* what a hunk of fly-blown little nothing England *is*!

Pause.

BERNARD. I'd like you to stay. In this flat, I mean.

CLAIRE. Look. All that stuff I dished you about wanting to lay me. I was *needling,* Bernard –

BERNARD. Well, I'm not talking about 'laying'. (*Pause.*) I'm worn out.

CLAIRE. By *what,* for Christ's sake?

Pause.

BERNARD. By feeling barren.

CLAIRE. And do I make you feel less barren, Bernard?

Pause.

BERNARD. Yes. I think you do.

CLAIRE. And what about the small noise shit and spit machine upstairs?

Pause.

BERNARD. I don't mind Rass –

CLAIRE. You don't *mind* him?

BERNARD. I mean –

CLAIRE. *I* mind him! I resent every subatomic particle *in* the little bastard.

Pause.

BERNARD (*quietly*). You *are* married to Haggerty? Aren't you?

Pause.

CLAIRE. Yes. Only I don't call it being married. I call it being shredded. Cell by goddam cell. (*Pause.*) So I usually deny the mind-stopping fact. A passion so aberrated and inexplicable as I had for Haggerty... I mean, the *scale* of the outrage to self-interest... it still surprises me. It's the only *surprise*... of which I am still capable.

BERNARD. Passion you had – or have for Haggerty?

He touches her face. She shakes away his hand. She is crying.

CLAIRE. I don't *know* Bernard –

Pause.

BERNARD. I've no passion (*Pause.*) You touch me.

Pause.

CLAIRE. Like your father touches you?

Pause.

BERNARD (*stiffly*). We'll leave it all alone then. (*He goes and sits down.*) Let it be.

Pause.

CLAIRE. What do you think *I* need? (*She gets up, walking up and down.*) I mean, *I've* had enough! (*Pause.*) The American *experience* they call it! Guys like you sitting round some studio table on British TV – *opining*, Bernard. *Pontificating*. Specialists in American affairs and God knows what. Washington, Chicago, Oakland, Detroit, Haarlem. Haggerty slipped through it all like some big bombed-out cat. Never a public figure, or a face. No pushing the Haggerty charisma, not on *your* life. Guts I don't need to prove, says he. Strategy. Tactics. Let the black-brained whites and the white-brained blacks boil it up, man. (*Pause.*) Weapons. Organization. (*Pause.*) And books and more books. Whilst little orphan white-fanny me! (*Pause.*) Exactly what are you implying that you are proposing, Bernard? I live here till we sink into some sort of tender stagnation? Waiting for the apocalypse? (*Pause.*) I've got money, energy. I've got fury, intelligence. I am *informed* out of my mind! I am warped beyond recognition, when I recall the infatuated buffoon slipped out father's ludicrous apartment overlooking Central Park. (*Pause.*) The way he fought it was pretty good. No nonsense with attorneys and the law and the fuzz. No. Just

an emanating centre of *hurt*. Of *pain*. Just a quiet unremitting
bombardment of *feeling* over there on Central Park. That I had
killed him long before he died. (*Pause.*) And to ram home the
point. When he *did* die. He left me pretty rich. (*Pause.*) The
machiavellian bastard! (*Pause.*) Knowing of course that living
with Haggerty it was a point of doctrine to live poor. I mean on
my part. Haggerty himself was as unaffected by the availability
of money as he was by the absence of it. (*Pause.*) You want *me*,
Bernard?

    Pause.

BERNARD. Living here. (*Pause.*) And then. You never know.

    Pause.

CLAIRE. I guess the first thing is to sit it out until Haggerty's
guy in Paris has carried out all his instructions. Huh?

    Pause.

How can *you* make *me* cry?

    Pause.

BERNARD. Just do as you like.

    She looks at her watch.

CLAIRE. It's nearly four. Where do you suppose Sawdust and
Tinsel have got to? I offered them lunch. No, said Chris. We'll
go round to the pub. (*Pause.*) *I* think that boy's a killer lost his
vocation!

    Pause.

BERNARD. The work's finished. (*Pause.*) I asked them round for
a drink about six. (*Pause.*) Have a drink. Give them a few
quid bonus in cash. (*Pause.*) Have a few drinks –

    Pause.

CLAIRE. I'm going up and talk to your father. You stabbed at him
good and hard, Bernard –

    Pause.

BERNARD. Do you feel anything about me?

CLAIRE. Yeah. You make me feel you've decided to be old.
Which makes me feel *older*.

    CLAIRE *exits. The outside doorbell rings.* BERNARD *goes to*

answer it. After a moment he comes back carrying a wreath.
There is an envelope pinned to it, with a card inside. He takes
out the card and reads:

BERNARD (*reading*). Bernard, man – I am not dead yet. I guess I
imagined that out of either depression or apoplexy, you might
now be ready to drape this round some cat's neck. (*Pause.*)
Your well-wisher: Haggerty.

BERNARD *picks up the wreath, sets it down on a chair in a*
corner. Goes out.

Fade out and fade in to

Scene Seven

Darkness. Two signs are lowered, one saying: AMAGANSETT, LONG
ISLAND; *the other –* CRANTHORPE, YORKSHIRE.

Two chairs: in one, BERNARD. *In the other,* CLAIRE.

A moving, dappled green and yellow light shifts across CLAIRE.
BERNARD *is in a glaring white spot.*

Before she speaks, we hear sea sounds: Before he speaks, we hear the
rattle and clatter of a pit.

CLAIRE. I don't care what you say, Haggerty. I shall hang on to
this place till the day I die. (*Pause.*) I spent my summers here.
(*Pause.*) I would like to have my baby here. (*Pause.*) Yes. And
we'll go to Europe because we go where you say.

Pause.

BERNARD. You've said everything you think about drinking to
me, dad, except *why*. For which thank God because the problem
has had me and my psycho-analyst ruminating for a number of
years. (*Pause.*) No, dad, I am *not* an out-patient at a mental
hospital. I am *not* in danger of what you would call insanity.
(*Pause.*) I lie on this man's couch in his consulting room and I
talk. (*Pause.*) Or I'm silent. (*Pause.*) Or I go to sleep. (*Pause.*)
What? Three guineas a session. (*Pause.*) Five days a week.
(*Pause.*) Yes. I am well aware that that adds up to three times

F

your pension. (*Pause.*) The idea, dad, is to penetrate the enigma
that is Bernard. (*Pause.*) What's that? (*Pause.*) And bloody good
luck to you too!

Pause.

CLAIRE. In my seventh month, Haggerty, I shall come back to
America and have your child here.

Pause.

BERNARD. Well. I send you ten quid a week, don't I? And I live
on forty. (*Pause.*) So I suppose I must make sixty-odd quid
a week. (*Pause.*) Nothing, dad. You fell asleep. I was just
mumbling to myself, having failed to notice that you had with-
drawn that minimal animation which passes for unconsciousness
in you.

Pause.

CLAIRE. It seems like I cannot remember the pre-Haggerty uni-
verse.

Pause.

BERNARD. Yes, I remember. God, I remember. The first slum.
The second slum. (*Pause.*) Then the first council house. (*Pause.*)
Hitler, Mussolini, Len Hutton. (*Pause.*) Yes, I remember you
used to take me up on the footplate. (*Pause.*) And let me press
the button on the coal hopper at the sheds on wage days. (*Pause.*)
Yes. Considering the historical conditions of the period, as the
comrades used to put it . . . yes, I had a happy childhood.
(*Pause.*) I *did* love my mother. (*Pause.*) But I only discovered that
when she was dead. (*Pause.*) I believe that is not uncommon dad.

CLAIRE. I know you'll leave me, Haggerty. Yes, I know. (*Pause.*)
Sometime. (*Pause.*) I have known this from the beginning.
(*Pause.*) That's a lot of years of wanting it in one way and fear-
ing it in another.

Pause.

BERNARD. Somehow, I didn't know *you* till she died.

CLAIRE. I know one day you will simply disappear. (*Pause.*) You
will have planned it.

Pause.

BERNARD. And now – it's too late.

CLAIRE. I should think it will be after the child is born. (*Pause.*) You'll want to be sure I have the real live thing kicking in my arms.

BERNARD. Blame? Blame you? (*Pause.*) For what?

CLAIRE. I'm going down by the sea, Haggerty. Walk by the sea. (*Pause.*) Watch the rollers.

Pause.

BERNARD. I'm moving again. (*Pause.*) To Hampstead. There's a bit of garden. A garden flat. (*Pause.*) Come down –

Pause.

CLAIRE. Out of this house. Through the woods. (*Pause.*) Only for a couple of hours. (*Pause.*) I don't want you to see one single more tear on my face! (*She stands.*)

BERNARD (*standing*). You could plant me a few flowers. (*Pause.*) Yes. Daffodils, if you like. (*Pause.*) Will the time come when it doesn't end up with you crying? (*Pause.*) Did you never want to cry when she was *alive?*

The spots go out. The signs raised.

Scene Eight

Fade up on: MR LINK in his chair. BERNARD sitting on his swivel chair by the desk. CLAIRE right of MR LINK. CHRIS left of MR LINK – both seated. ROGER standing. They all have drinks and there is a trolley with bottles, glasses, ice, etc. MR LINK has a glass of Guinness. The others whisky or vodka. There is an uncomfortable silence for some time.

FATHER. You'll be moving on to another job, then. Chris and Roger. (*Raises his glass.*) Good health –

Pause.

ROGER. Not me I won't. I've got the sack.

FATHER. I'm sorry about that, young man. But it isn't as if it was your trade. Now, is it?

ROGER. Oh, absolutely! Just a question of body and soul being kept together, that's all.

Long pause. FATHER *looks round.*

FATHER. There in't nobody gives you a good job for your money nowdays. No pride in what they do. Chuck it together, grab your brass and off.

CHRIS *stands, goes to* MR LINK.

CHRIS. You dissatisfied with what we done with Bernard's place?

Pause.

FATHER. I was speaking generally, young man. Don't take it personal.

CHRIS. Right. (*He turns and moves away a little.*)

FATHER. Mind. When you come to look round. When you take a *close* look. It's cheap paint. And where there's wood – cheap wood. (*Pause.*) Don't reckon much to t'grouting on them bath-room tiles, neither.

CHRIS *rounds on him.*

CHRIS. We done a thorough job! And listened to *you* drivellin' on for hours into the bargain –

Pause.

FATHER. Bernard. Are you going to let this one speak like this to me in your own house?

BERNARD. Chris –

CHRIS. I run away from one like you, Mr Link. Just like you, an' a dirty southerner *into the bargain.* With you it's all up north and pre-war and this and that and the other. With him it was Dunkirk. El Alamein to Rome! But you're all the same. You're all bloody fossils! And we different and you don't like it. You sneer and mumble at what we wear, what we do, how we feel, how we screw. (*Pause.*) Well, I'll say to you what I said to him: *screw you!* (*He drains his glass and puts it down.*) Sorry, Ber-nard –

FATHER. Now that's a bit on a mystery, that is –

Pause.

ROGER. No mystery about it, dear! Just try not to get upset, that's all. What's Chrissy to *you*?

   Pause.

FATHER. He 'ad *me* deceived at first. I thowt he were t'best on the two of you. (*Pause.*) You being like, an *amateur* Roger –

ROGER. Thanks ever so!

BERNARD. Dad, you don't know a thing about interior decorating, or carpentry, or any of it.

ROGER. And I suppose you think *I'm* inferior because I'm queer! Don't you worry, Father Bear – the *'omo* is *off*. Not going to hang round listening to –

FATHER (*cutting in*). I know *quality* when I see it, Bernard. Quality of *workmanship*.

ROGER. I only stuck it out for Bernard's sake –

FATHER. Aye. I'm not surprised to 'ear that, neither.

   BERNARD *gets up and goes to his father.*

BERNARD. And what do you mean by *that*?

   Pause.

FATHER. Manly is as manly does.

ROGER. God, he's awful! I mean I thought he was lovely and primitive and quaint when he arrived. (*Going to* FATHER.) My Link, you're a nasty destructive old man. And your Bernard's *'etero* – though I don't suppose you'll get that because it isn't a soap powder, is it?

   ROGER *slams down his drink and flounces out.* BERNARD *takes the chair occupied by* CHRIS. ROGER *pops his head back round the door.*

ROGER. More's the pity, Bernard – (*And withdraws again, closing the door.*)

   Long pause.

BERNARD. Thanks very much, father.

FATHER. No point in bottling owt up.

   Pause.

BERNARD. We were supposed to be having a friendly drink before they left!

FATHER. *Friendly drink!* Have you seen yon ceiling in t'baby's room? (*Pause.*) It could come down, that ceiling could. Aye. An' wi' a bairn underneath. I give it a prod, an' all flakes come down. What they've done, they've licked a bit of paint over rotten plaster. (*Pause.*) It's the modern way, in't it? (*Pause.*) That doesn't mean you've got to keep your mouth shut.

CLAIRE. Mr Link. Chris went over the place and made a list of everything needed doing. Then he did what Bernard said he could afford. What he did seems pretty good to me. D'you think *I* don't know the condition of this apartment? I lived here long enough!

Pause.

FATHER. Our Bernard. He won't speak up for his own good –

BERNARD. No. He's not manly enough, isn't our Bernard.

FATHER. Well, I'm right, aren't I? You've never been what I'd call a man. And if I see summat wrong when I'm down in London, well, I try to put it right. You won't speak up for yoursen. You'd let 'em rob t'shirt off your back. Is *that* manly?

Pause.

BERNARD. No, dad.

Pause.

FATHER. *Always* been a weakling. (*Pause: to* CLAIRE.) He run away from t'Germans, you know. In t'war. Got a scar on his backside the size of a bakin' tin. (*Pause.*) His mother was a fine woman, but I always thought there was summat wrong on her side on t'family. More than one bad 'un. Who handed out t'half-crown pieces every time when her brothers were locked out on t'pit? Me. Muggins. (*Pause.*) He's picked summat up from her side, Bernard has. (*Pause.*) She had all the good on her side on t'family in *her*, his mother did. God rest her.

Pause.

CLAIRE (*standing*). I guess I'm moving over the other side of the barricade from you, Mr Link. Reluctantly, but you sure do provoke! I thought it was just Bernard needled *you*. (*Pause.*) What's the matter with you, Mr Link?

FATHER. Nothing's wrong wi' me, love. (*Drains his glass.*) I'm fine. Fit as a lop. (*Pause.*) I'm used to people taking against me. We very blunt you know, in Yorkshire. Blunt but straight. Straight as a die.

CLAIRE. Anybody in Yorkshire take against you?

MR LINK *slowly swivels his head, to where he can see the wreath standing in a corner.*

FATHER. Might I ask what a wreath's doing in the house?
Pause.

CLAIRE. My husband sent it.

FATHER. Oh. He did, did he? Somebody kicked t'bucket, like?

CLAIRE. No, Mr Link. He has a kind of morbid sense of humour.
Pause.

FATHER (*slowly*). Is there owt funny goin' on, then?

CLAIRE. Not a thing.
Pause.

FATHER. There's another one wasting his brass then. In't there? (*Pause.*) I was hoping we'd have a bit on a talk one of these days. About your husband. (*Pause.*) I'd have that baby's name changed by deed poll if I was you. You can do it, you know. It might be a quid or two. But he can't go to school wi' that name – can he? Bernard said it come out on some book or other.

CLAIRE. That's right. (*Pause.*) A book called 'Crime and Punishment'.
Pause.

FATHER. That in't a morbid sense of 'umour! More like a screw loose, in't it?

CLAIRE (*drily*). Haggerty is as Haggerty does, Mr Link –
Pause.

FATHER. Aye. Everyman's the right to be master in his own house. (*Pause.*) Except o' course, he's nowhere to be seen. (*Pause.*) The way they split up nowadays! What do they get married *for*?
Pause.

CLAIRE (*quietly and deliberately*). Well, you see, Mr Link. I married Haggerty when I was very young. And I had absorbed the beliefs of my parents –

FATHER (*cutting in*). That's right an' all. It's in the Commandments. Honour thy father and thy mother that thy days shall be long in the land which the Lord thy God giveth thee.

Pause.

CLAIRE. Yes. (*Pause.*) Very well put, Mr Link. Only I came unstuck because you see I sort of had the Commandments on the one hand, and the desire to fuck Haggerty day and night on the other.

BERNARD'S *father is stunned. His glass drops out of his hand.*

FATHER. Bernard – I'm not stopping here another minute!

Long pause.

BERNARD. I don't see you moving, dad.

FATHER. Did you hear what she *said*?

BERNARD. Yes. *Isn't* she a dirty-mouthed bitch! After all?

FATHER (*to* CLAIRE). I'm afraid that that is what I think you are, young woman! I've never heard the like –

Pause.

BERNARD. Still sitting there, dad –

Long pause.

FATHER. I'll shift when *I'm* ready. And it'll be for good, I can tell thee!

BERNARD *goes to the wreath, picks it up. Holds it, looking at it.*

BERNARD. What size do you take dad? Shirt collar?

FATHER (*caught off balance*). Eh?

BERNARD. Size of shirt collar?

FATHER. Seventeen an' a half. But –

BERNARD (*cutting in*). Yes. Well, I think it might fit.

He walks to his father, holds the wreath over his head and slowly places it down over his shoulders.

FATHER (*half rising*). What the bloody hell –

BERNARD *puts his hands on his father's shoulders and firmly presses him back into the chair.*

BERNARD. No. Don't move, dad. Too old to change your habits now. (*Pause.*) It looks well on you.

> CLAIRE *can't take this, she turns away. Slowly* MR LINK *rises to his feet – dazed, clutching at the wreath but holding it in position.*

FATHER (*almost crying*). Eh, Bernard –

> *Pause.*

BERNARD. Cruel?

FATHER. *Bernard –*

BERNARD. Not comical?

> *Pause.*

FATHER. *Bernard –*

BERNARD. Bear up. Remember one of your many hundreds of banal remarks. Oft repeated. (*Pause.*) A nod's as good as a wink to a blind donkey –

> MR LINK, *trance-like, pulls the wreath off and throws it down. He looks at his feet.*

FATHER. I'm an old man. And your father.

> *Pause.*

BERNARD. Yes. You are.

> *Pause.*

FATHER. I should be respected.

BERNARD. Yes. You should be respected.

> *Pause.*

FATHER. I'll have no more on thee!

> *Pause.*

BERNARD. I've had enough of you.

> *Pause.*

FATHER. You should be ashamed.

BERNARD. I *am* ashamed.

FATHER (*shouting*). I'll strike thee down!

> *Pause.*

BERNARD. Strike me –

> *Pause.*

FATHER. I'll not touch thee. I'll not mucky my hands.

Pause.

BERNARD. You never *have touched* me.

Pause.

FATHER (*now crying*). I've loved my son.

BERNARD. Undetectably.

Pause.

FATHER. I've failed thee? Some road?

Pause.

BERNARD. No, father.

Pause.

FATHER. So . . . tha loved only thy mother!

BERNARD. No, father. I loved you as well.

Pause.

FATHER. What did I do to harm thee? I worked mesen dead.
Come home nearly too tired to eat. Fell into t'chair by the fire.
(*Pause.*) And went to bed when I woke up.

He stands a moment, rubbing his eyes.

You an' your mother was always chattering away. (*Shouts.*) I
know I niver had nowt to say!

Pause.

BERNARD. Shall we say, father . . . that after your fashion, you
became eloquent once she was dead? (*Pause.*) It was high time
somebody flung a wreath on you.

Pause.

FATHER. I can't make nowt on any on this.

BERNARD. There's nowhere to begin. Is there?

Pause.

FATHER. You've broken my pride this day.

BERNARD *simply stands staring at him. His* FATHER *looks
pleadingly towards* CLAIRE, *but her back is turned.*

MR LINK *slowly shuffles to the stairs door and goes out, closing
it quietly behind him.* CLAIRE *goes to* BERNARD.

CLAIRE. *Are* you ashamed?

BERNARD. Yes.

Pause.

CLAIRE. But you could go through with that –

BERNARD. You didn't make a bad start yourself.

Pause.

CLAIRE. I'm more ashamed than you are.

She sinks into one of the chairs, her face in her hands. BERNARD *remains standing. The doorbell rings.* CLAIRE *takes no notice. After a moment,* BERNARD *goes out to answer it. There is a mumble of voices in the hall. Two men walk in through the hall door carrying a coffin.* BERNARD *follows them helplessly.*

BERNARD. I tell you you've come to the wrong place –

FIRST MAN. No, we 'aven't, sir.

SECOND MAN (*holds out a piece of paper*). It's your address, sir. And the order was from the agent of a Mr Haggerty in Paris –

FIRST MAN. Nobody dead in the house? Well, it's an *empty* one, sir. Must be a joke –

He laughs half-heartedly. CLAIRE *is sitting up staring horrified at the coffin. The two men go out.*

SECOND MAN (*leaving*). There's a plaque and some writing on it, Mr Link. (*Exits.*)

CLAIRE (*sharply*). Read it out, Bernard –

Pause.

BERNARD. You read it. (*Pause.*) It's none of my affair.

BERNARD *goes out through the hall door, pulling his jacket off a chair as he goes.* CLAIRE *slowly approaches the coffin. She kneels beside it and reads out slowly:*

CLAIRE (*reading*). There's more to this box

> Than macabre wit.
> Haggerty's dead
> But he's not in it.

Pause.

> Bury it some place
> If you have a mind.
> The rightful contents
> Would be hard to find.

Pause.

James Mawnan Haggerty. Guerrilla. Killed during a skirmish between Government Forces and a rebel unit. Africa. Nineteen seventy.

    CLAIRE *stays beside the coffin for some moments. She gets up. Looks round. Sees the wreath on the floor. She picks it up and drops it on the coffin. Exits through the door to the stairs. Curtain.*

    The coffin remains downstage of the curtain.

Methuen's Modern Plays

Paul Ableman	*Green Julia*
Jean Anouilh	*Antigone*
	Becket
	The Lark
	The Director of the Opera
John Arden	*Serjeant Musgrave's Dance*
	The Workhouse Donkey
	Armstrong's Last Goodnight
John Arden and	*The Business of Good Government*
Margaretta D'Arcy	*The Royal Pardon*
	The Hero Rises Up
	The Island of the Mighty
Wolfgang Bauer,	*Shakespeare the Sadist,*
Rainer Werner Fassbinder,	*Bremen Coffee,*
Peter Handke,	*My Foot My Tutor,*
Franz Xaver Kroetz	*Stallerhof*
Brendan Behan	*The Quare Fellow*
	The Hostage
	Richard's Cork Leg
Edward Bond	*Saved*
	Narrow Road to the Deep North
	The Pope's Wedding
	Lear
	The Sea
	Bingo
	The Fool and *We Come to the River*
	Theatre Poems and Songs
	The Bundle
John Bowen	*Little Boxes*
Bertolt Brecht	*Mother Courage*
	The Caucasian Chalk Circle
	The Good Person of Szechwan
	The Life of Galileo
	The Threepenny Opera
	Saint Joan of the Stockyards
	The Resistible Rise of Arturo Ui
	The Mother
	Mr Puntila and His Man Matti
	The Measures Taken and other Lehrstücke
	The Days of the Commune
	The Messingkauf Dialogues
	Man Equals Man and *The Elephant Calf*
	The Rise and Fall of the City of Mahagonny and *The Seven Deadly Sins*
Howard Brenton	*The Churchill Play*
	Weapons of Happiness
	Epsom Downs
Howard Brenton and David Hare	*Brassneck*
Syd Cheatle	*Straight Up*
Shelagh Delaney	*A Taste of Honey*

David Edgar	*Destiny*
Michael Frayn	*Clouds*
	Alphabetical Order and *Donkeys' Years*
Max Frisch	*The Fire Raisers*
	Andorra
Jean Giraudoux	*Tiger at the Gates*
Simon Gray	*Butley*
	Otherwise Engaged and other plays
	Dog Days
	The Rear Column and other plays
Peter Handke	*Offending the Audience* and *Self-Accusation*
	Kaspar
	The Ride Across Lake Constance
	They Are Dying Out
Barrie Keeffe	*Gimme Shelter*
	Barbarians
Arthur Kopit	*Indians*
David Mercer	*On the Eve of Publication*
	After Haggerty
	Flint
	The Bankrupt and other plays
	Duck Song
	Huggy Bear and other plays
John Mortimer	*The Judge*
	Five Plays
	Come As You Are
	A Voyage Round My Father
	Collaborators
Joe Orton	*Crimes of Passion*
	Loot
	What the Butler Saw
	Funeral Games and *The Good and Faithful Servant*
	Entertaining Mr Sloane
Harold Pinter	*The Birthday Party*
	The Room and *The Dumb Waiter*
	The Caretaker
	A Slight Ache and other plays
	The Collection and *The Lover*
	The Homecoming
	Tea Party and other plays
	Landscape and *Silence*
	Old Times
	No Man's Land
	Betrayal
Stephen Poliakoff	*Hitting Town* and *City Sugar*
Jean-Paul Sartre	*Crime Passionnel*
Wole Soyinka	*Madmen and Specialists*
	The Jero Plays
	Death and the King's Horseman
Theatre Workshop	*Oh What a Lovely War*
Boris Vian	*The Empire Builders*
Peter Weiss	*Trotsky in Exile*
Charles Wood	*'H'*
	Veterans
Carl Zuckmayer	*The Captain of Köpenick*

The Master Playwrights
from Eyre Methuen

Collections of plays by the best-known modern playwrights in value-for-money paperbacks.

John Arden
PLAYS: ONE
Serjeant Musgrave's Dance, The Workhouse Donkey, Armstrong's Last Goodnight

Brendan Behan
THE COMPLETE PLAYS
The Quare Fellow, The Hostage, Richard's Cork Leg, Moving Out, A Garden Party, The Big House

Edward Bond
PLAYS: ONE
The Pope's Wedding, Saved, Early Morning

PLAYS: TWO
Lear, The Sea, Narrow Road to the Deep North, Black Mass, Passion

Joe Orton
THE COMPLETE PLAYS
The Ruffian on the Stair, Entertaining Mr Sloane, Loot, The Erpingham Camp, The Good and Faithful Servant, Funeral Games, What the Butler Saw

Harold Pinter
PLAYS: ONE
The Room, The Dumb Waiter, The Birthday Party, A Slight Ache, A Night Out

PLAYS: TWO
The Caretaker, Night School, The Dwarfs, The Collection, The Lover

PLAYS: THREE
The Homecoming, Tea Party, The Basement, Landscape, Silence

Strindberg
THE FATHER, MISS JULIE AND THE GHOST SONATA
Translated with introductions by Michael Meyer

Methuen's New Theatrescripts

Theatrescripts aim to close the gap between the appearance of new work in the theatre and its publication in script form. The emphasis is on new or unconventional work, and the price is kept as low as possible.

EDWARD BOND
A-A-America! *and* Stone

ANDREY AMALRIK
East-West *and* Is Uncle Jack a Conformist?

DAVID CREGAN
Poor Tom *and* Tina

DAVID EDGAR
Wreckers

STEPHEN POLIAKOFF
Strawberry Fields

BARRIE KEEFFE
A Mad World My Masters

PETER CHEESEMAN (Ed.)
Fight for Shelton Bar

JOHN MACKENDRICK
Lavender Blue *and* Noli Me Tangere

DAVID MAMET
American Buffalo, Sexual Perversity in Chicago *and* Duck Variations

DENNIS POTTER
Brimstone and Treacle

If you would like regular information on new Methuen plays and theatre books, please write to:
The Marketing Department
Eyre Methuen Ltd
North Way
Andover
Hants